Breathe

JOURNEYS TO HEALTHY BINDING

For Amila, who gave me my first binder.
And for Phoebe, who helped me through top surgery.
Love you so much <3
~MAIA

To the members of the BREATHE cohort,
whose stories are woven together here, and whose tireless
participation made this research possible. Thank you for
imagining with us a world in which we can all breathe.
~SARAH

DUTTON BOOKS
An imprint of Penguin Random House LLC, New York

First published in the United States of America by Dutton Books,
an imprint of Penguin Random House LLC, 2024

Visit us online at PenguinRandomHouse.com.

Library of Congress Cataloging-in-Publication Data is available.

ISBN 9780593855836 (hardcover)
1 3 5 7 9 10 8 6 4 2

ISBN 9780593855829 (paperback)
1 3 5 7 9 10 8 6 4 2

Printed in the United States of America

WOR
Design by Maia Kobabe and Anna Booth
Color by Ashley R. Guillory
Text set in Avenir Next and Marker Felt Thin

This is a work of nonfiction. Some names and identifying details have been changed.

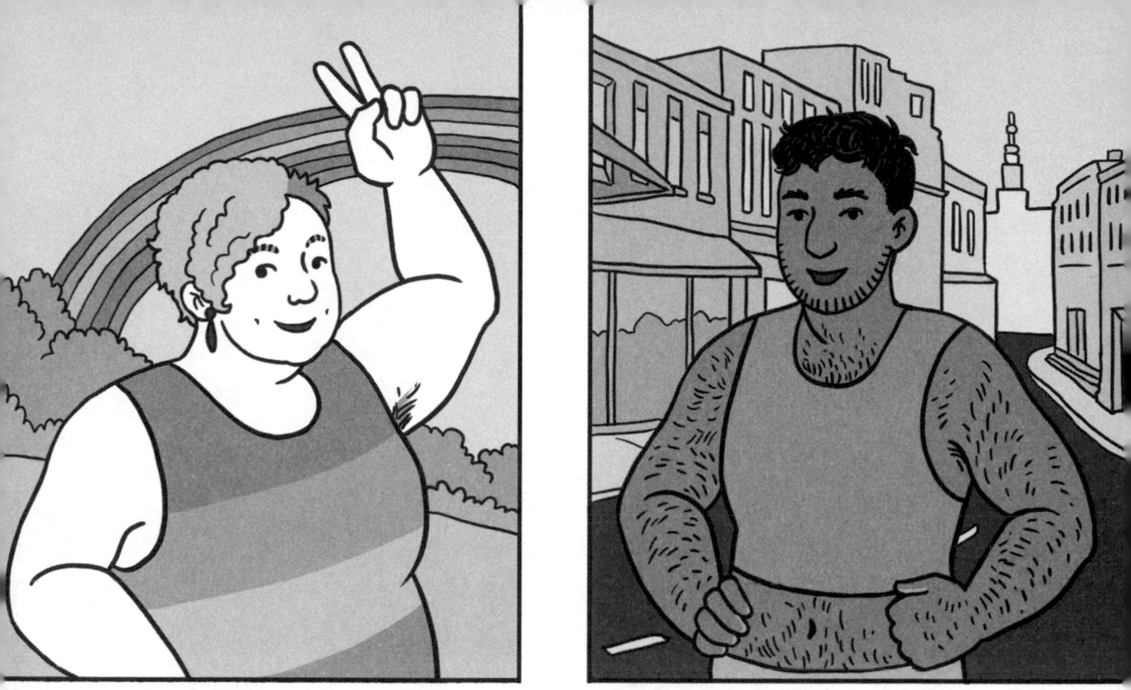

Breathe

JOURNEYS TO HEALTHY BINDING

by **Maia Kobabe** *and* **Sarah Peitzmeier, PhD**

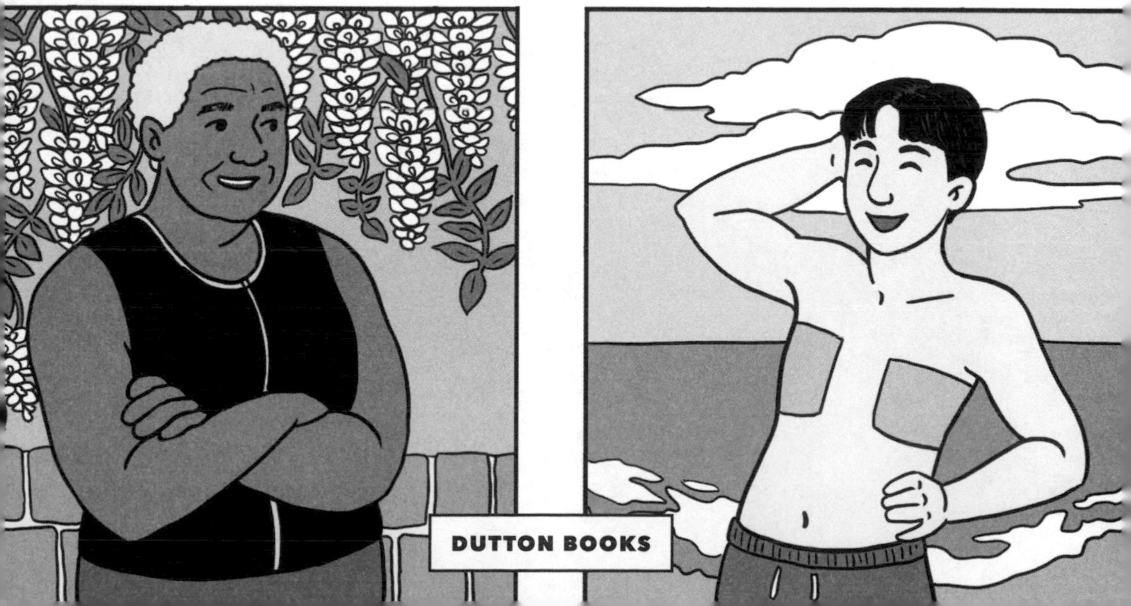

DUTTON BOOKS

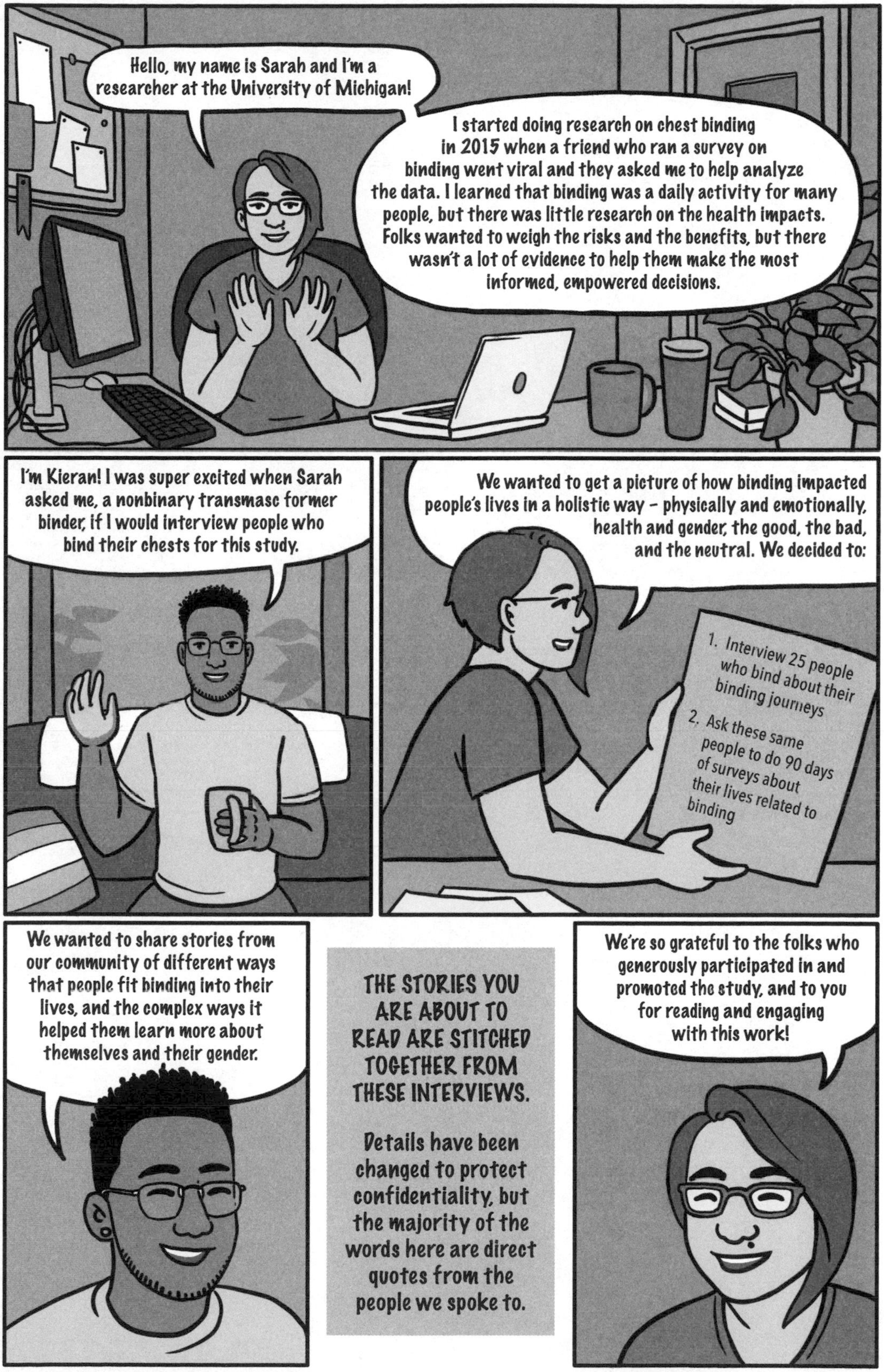
Hello, my name is Sarah and I'm a researcher at the University of Michigan!
I started doing research on chest binding in 2015 when a friend who ran a survey on binding went viral and they asked me to help analyze the data. I learned that binding was a daily activity for many people, but there was little research on the health impacts. Folks wanted to weigh the risks and the benefits, but there wasn't a lot of evidence to help them make the most informed, empowered decisions.
I'm Kieran! I was super excited when Sarah asked me, a nonbinary transmasc former binder, if I would interview people who bind their chests for this study.
We wanted to get a picture of how binding impacted people's lives in a holistic way - physically and emotionally, health and gender, the good, the bad, and the neutral. We decided to:
1. Interview 25 people who bind about their binding journeys
2. Ask these same people to do 90 days of surveys about their lives related to binding
We wanted to share stories from our community of different ways that people fit binding into their lives, and the complex ways it helped them learn more about themselves and their gender.
THE STORIES YOU ARE ABOUT TO READ ARE STITCHED TOGETHER FROM THESE INTERVIEWS.
Details have been changed to protect confidentiality, but the majority of the words here are direct quotes from the people we spoke to.
We're so grateful to the folks who generously participated in and promoted the study, and to you for reading and engaging with this work!

Binding Stories

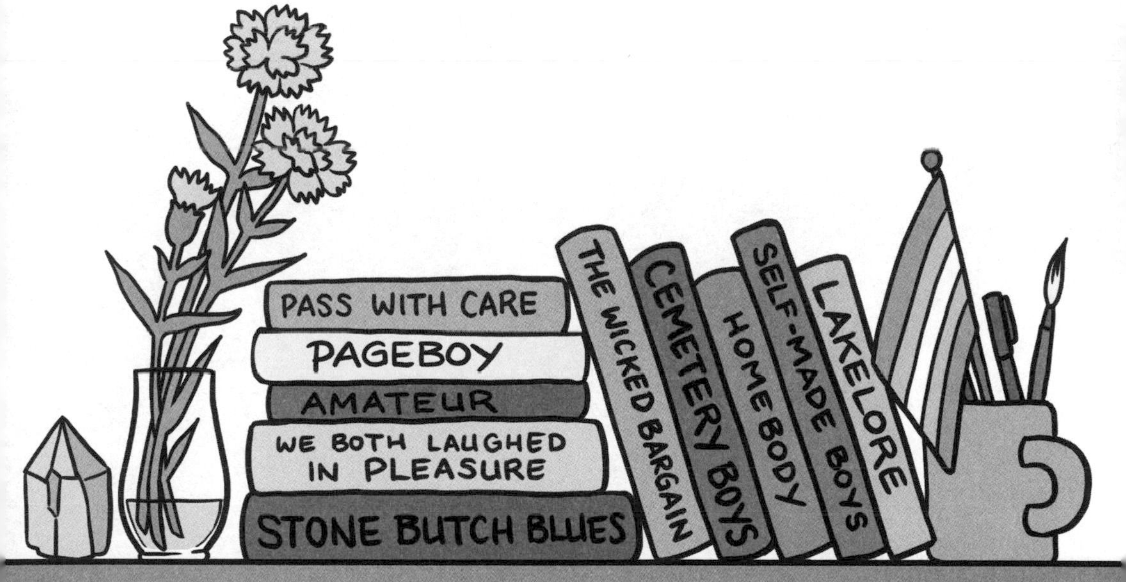
PASS WITH CARE
PAGEBOY
AMATEUR
WE BOTH LAUGHED IN PLEASURE
STONE BUTCH BLUES
THE WICKED BARGAIN
CEMETERY BOYS
HOME BODY
SELF-MADE BOYS
LAKELORE

A, 22 years old, they/she

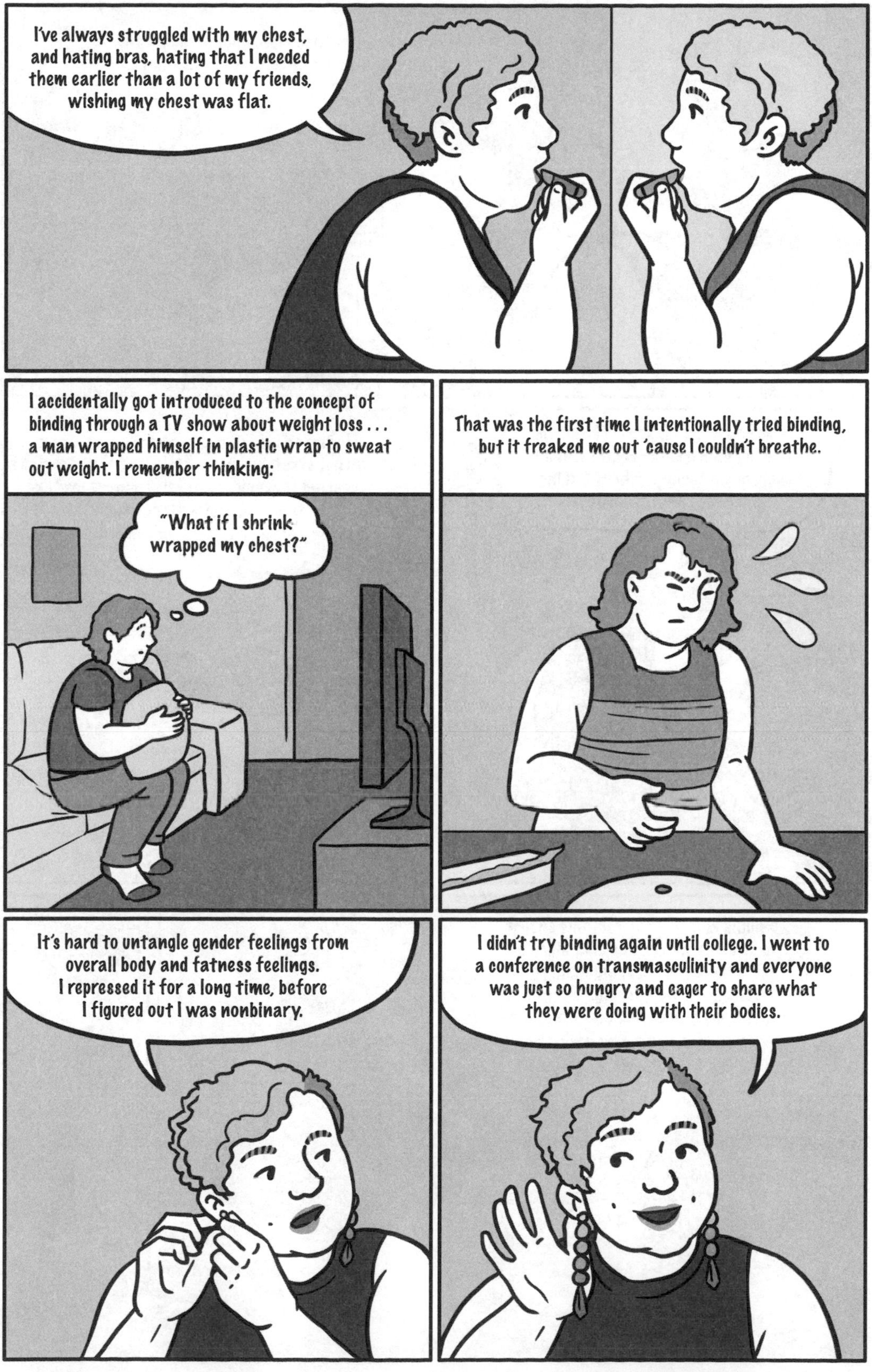
I've always struggled with my chest, and hating bras, hating that I needed them earlier than a lot of my friends, wishing my chest was flat.
I accidentally got introduced to the concept of binding through a TV show about weight loss . . . a man wrapped himself in plastic wrap to sweat out weight. I remember thinking:
"What if I shrink wrapped my chest?"
That was the first time I intentionally tried binding, but it freaked me out 'cause I couldn't breathe.
It's hard to untangle gender feelings from overall body and fatness feelings. I repressed it for a long time, before I figured out I was nonbinary.
I didn't try binding again until college. I went to a conference on transmasculinity and everyone was just so hungry and eager to share what they were doing with their bodies.

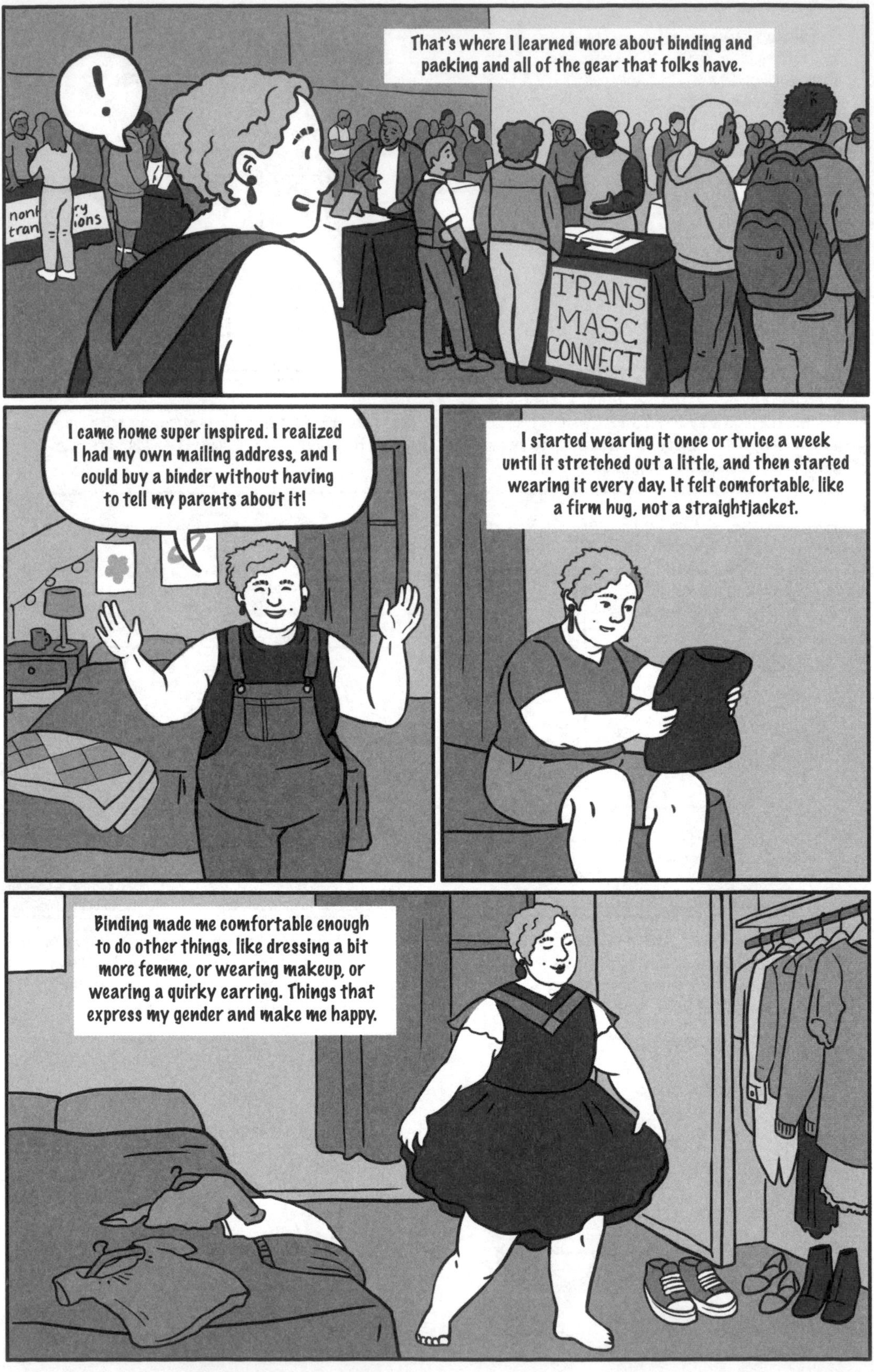
That's where I learned more about binding and packing and all of the gear that folks have.
!
TRANS MASC CONNECT
I came home super inspired. I realized I had my own mailing address, and I could buy a binder without having to tell my parents about it!
I started wearing it once or twice a week until it stretched out a little, and then started wearing it every day. It felt comfortable, like a firm hug, not a straightjacket.
Binding made me comfortable enough to do other things, like dressing a bit more femme, or wearing makeup, or wearing a quirky earring. Things that express my gender and make me happy.

I also joined my school's Frisbee team, which was VERY queer, VERY trans.

We were all binding, running around, and struggling to breathe. I'd get really hot, really short of breath, a lot of chafing . . .

But I really wanted to bind in this very queer space, even though it was a struggle!

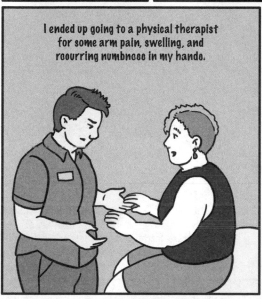

I ended up going to a physical therapist for some arm pain, swelling, and recurring numbness in my hands.

Please hold your hands in the air for 30 seconds.

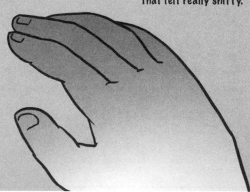

My hands turned purple and didn't come back for a long time. That shook me up. I showed my friends on the team, but if anything they just seemed impressed.

It was like the more my body hurt while playing, the more I was perceived as trans by my team.

That felt really shitty.

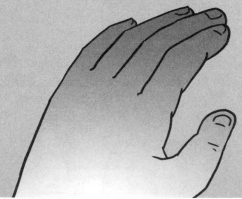

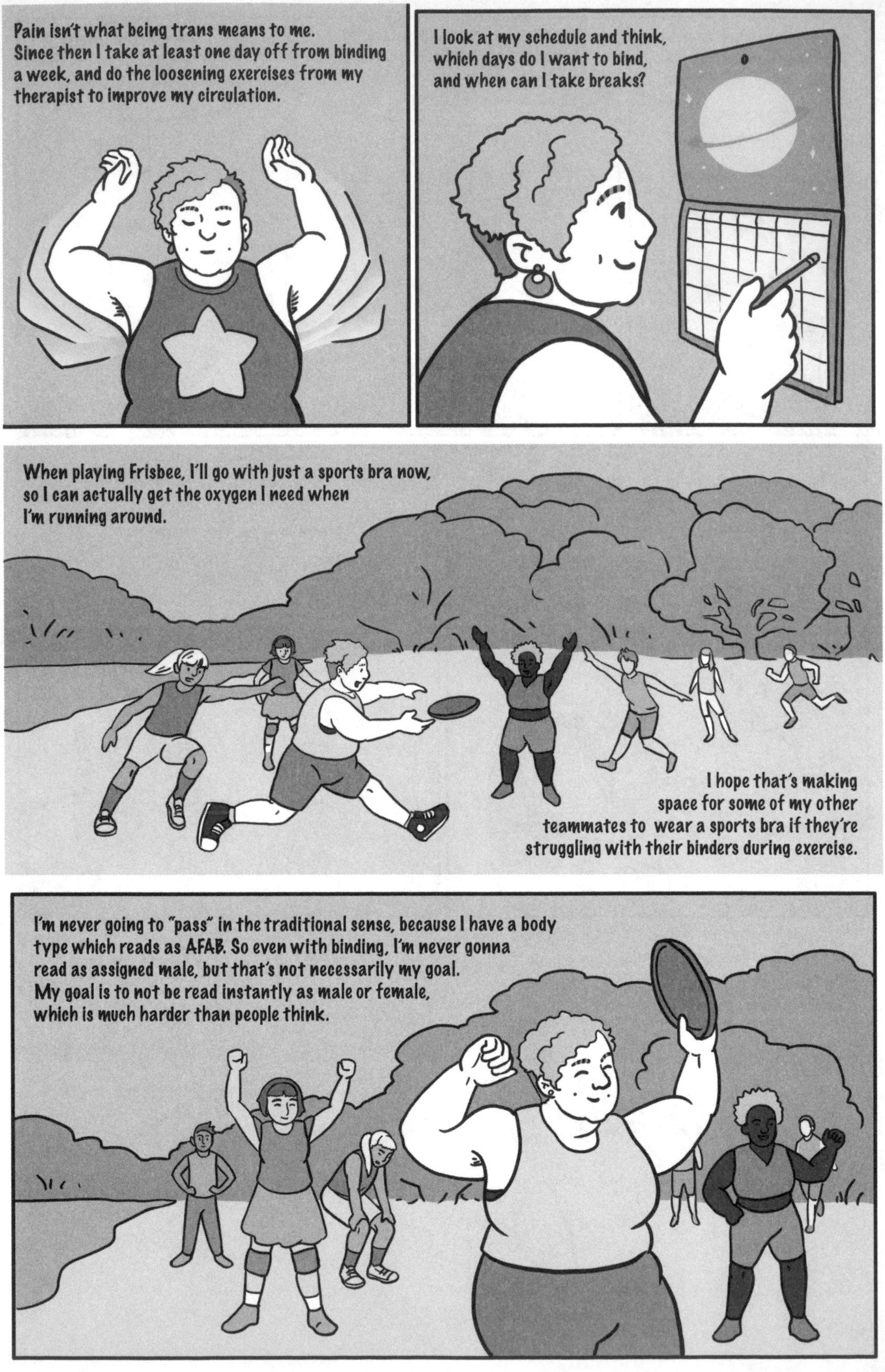
Pain isn't what being trans means to me.
Since then I take at least one day off from binding a week, and do the loosening exercises from my therapist to improve my circulation.
I look at my schedule and think, which days do I want to bind, and when can I take breaks?
When playing Frisbee, I'll go with just a sports bra now, so I can actually get the oxygen I need when I'm running around.
I hope that's making space for some of my other teammates to wear a sports bra if they're struggling with their binders during exercise.
I'm never going to "pass" in the traditional sense, because I have a body type which reads as AFAB. So even with binding, I'm never gonna read as assigned male, but that's not necessarily my goal.
My goal is to not be read instantly as male or female, which is much harder than people think.

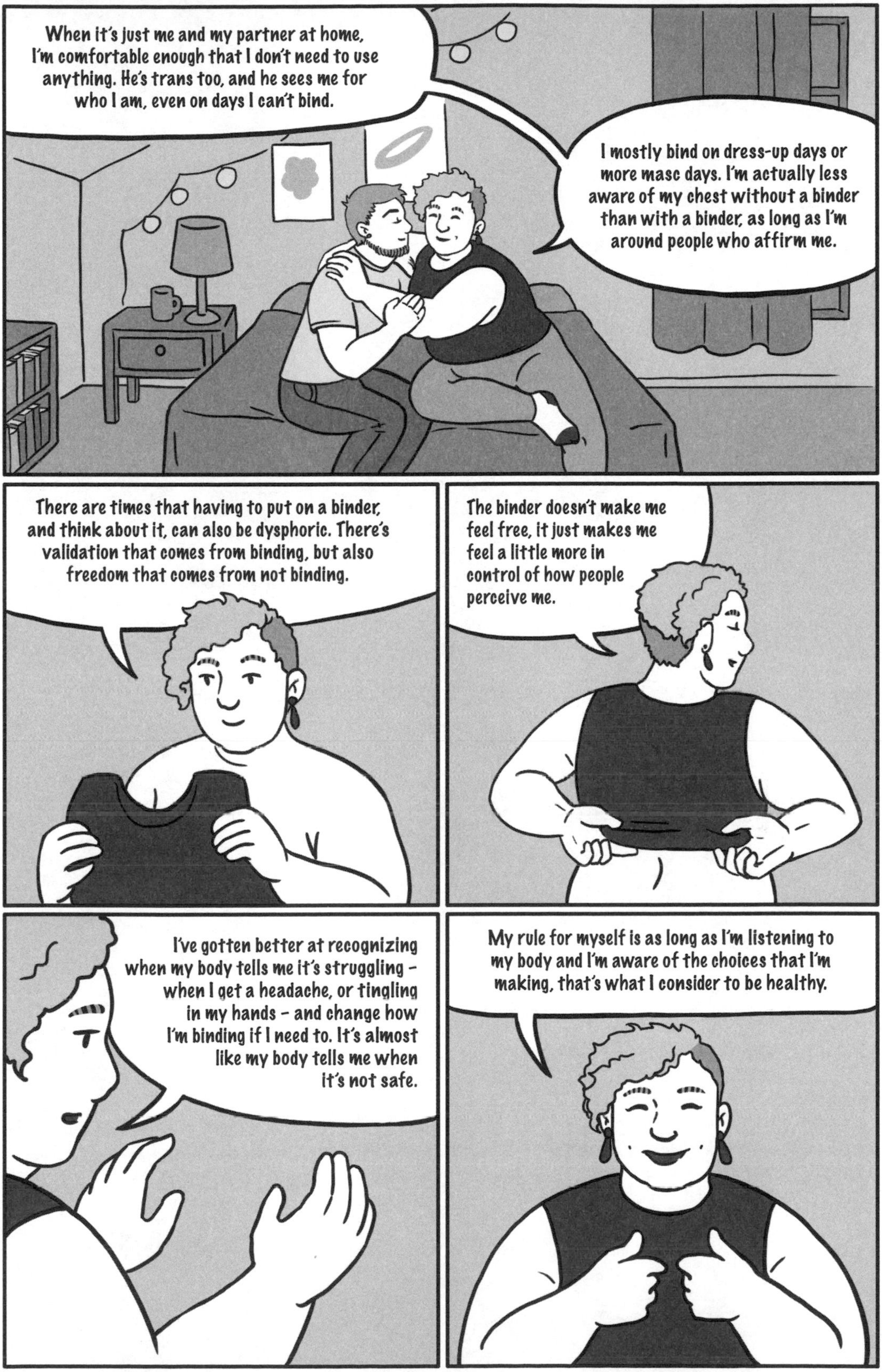
When it's just me and my partner at home, I'm comfortable enough that I don't need to use anything. He's trans too, and he sees me for who I am, even on days I can't bind.
I mostly bind on dress-up days or more masc days. I'm actually less aware of my chest without a binder than with a binder, as long as I'm around people who affirm me.
There are times that having to put on a binder, and think about it, can also be dysphoric. There's validation that comes from binding, but also freedom that comes from not binding.
The binder doesn't make me feel free, it just makes me feel a little more in control of how people perceive me.
I've gotten better at recognizing when my body tells me it's struggling – when I get a headache, or tingling in my hands – and change how I'm binding if I need to. It's almost like my body tells me when it's not safe.
My rule for myself is as long as I'm listening to my body and I'm aware of the choices that I'm making, that's what I consider to be healthy.

B, 30 years old, he/him

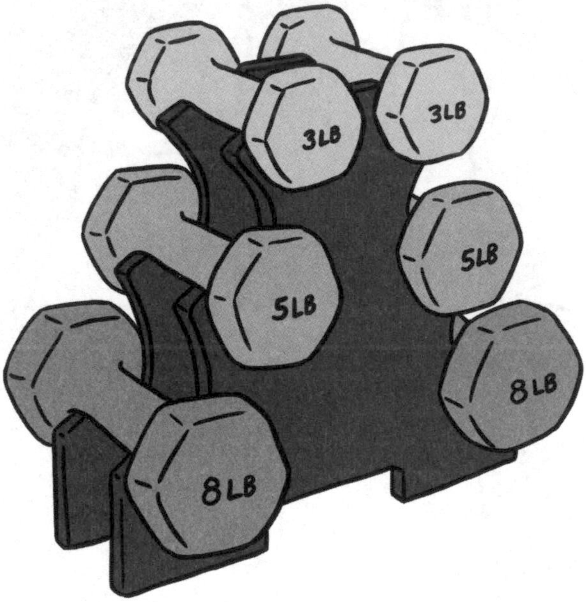
3LB
3LB
5LB
5LB
8LB
8LB

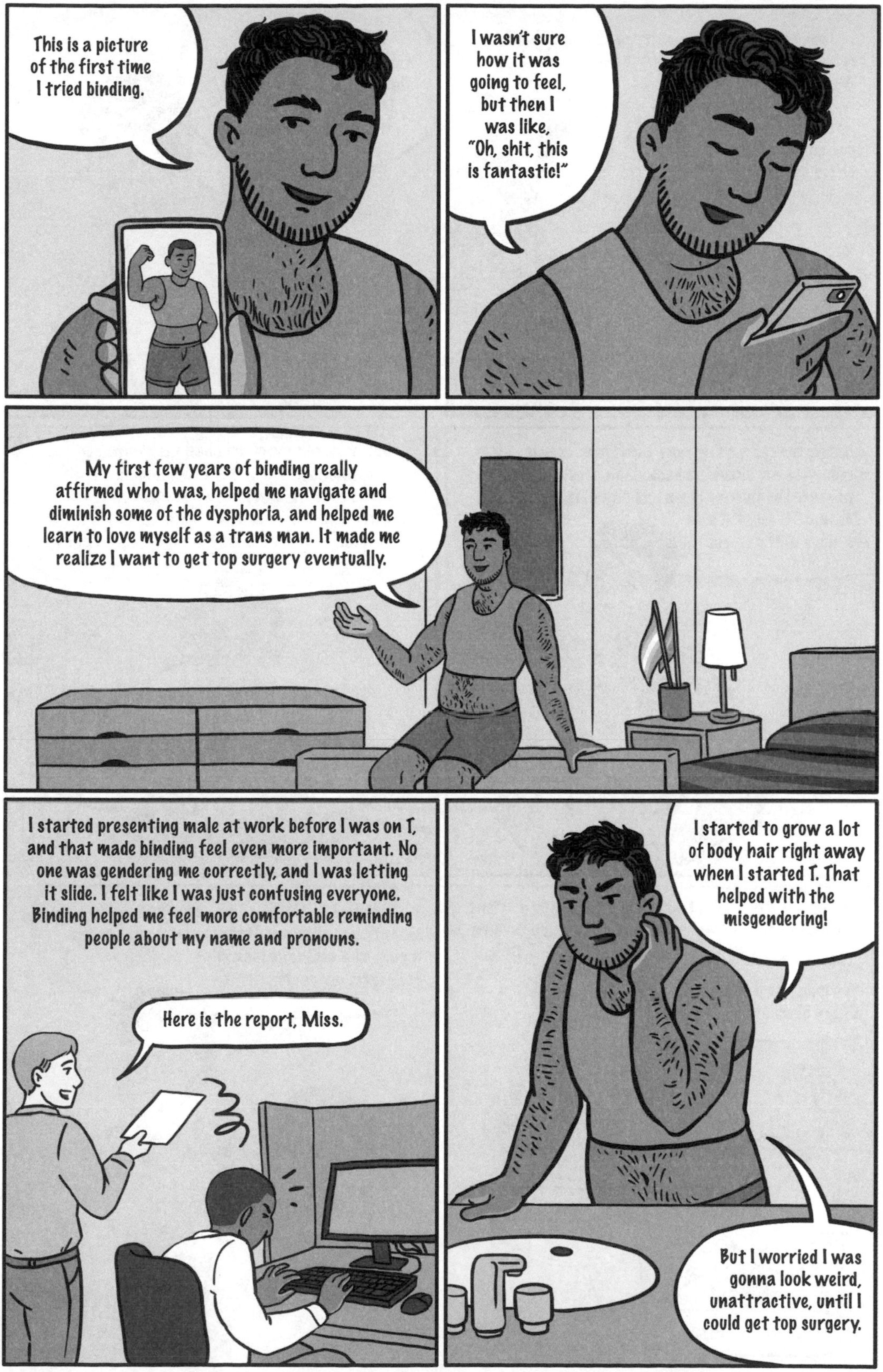
This is a picture of the first time I tried binding.
I wasn't sure how it was going to feel, but then I was like, "Oh, shit, this is fantastic!"
My first few years of binding really affirmed who I was, helped me navigate and diminish some of the dysphoria, and helped me learn to love myself as a trans man. It made me realize I want to get top surgery eventually.
I started presenting male at work before I was on T, and that made binding feel even more important. No one was gendering me correctly, and I was letting it slide. I felt like I was just confusing everyone. Binding helped me feel more comfortable reminding people about my name and pronouns.
Here is the report, Miss.
I started to grow a lot of body hair right away when I started T. That helped with the misgendering!
But I worried I was gonna look weird, unattractive, until I could get top surgery.

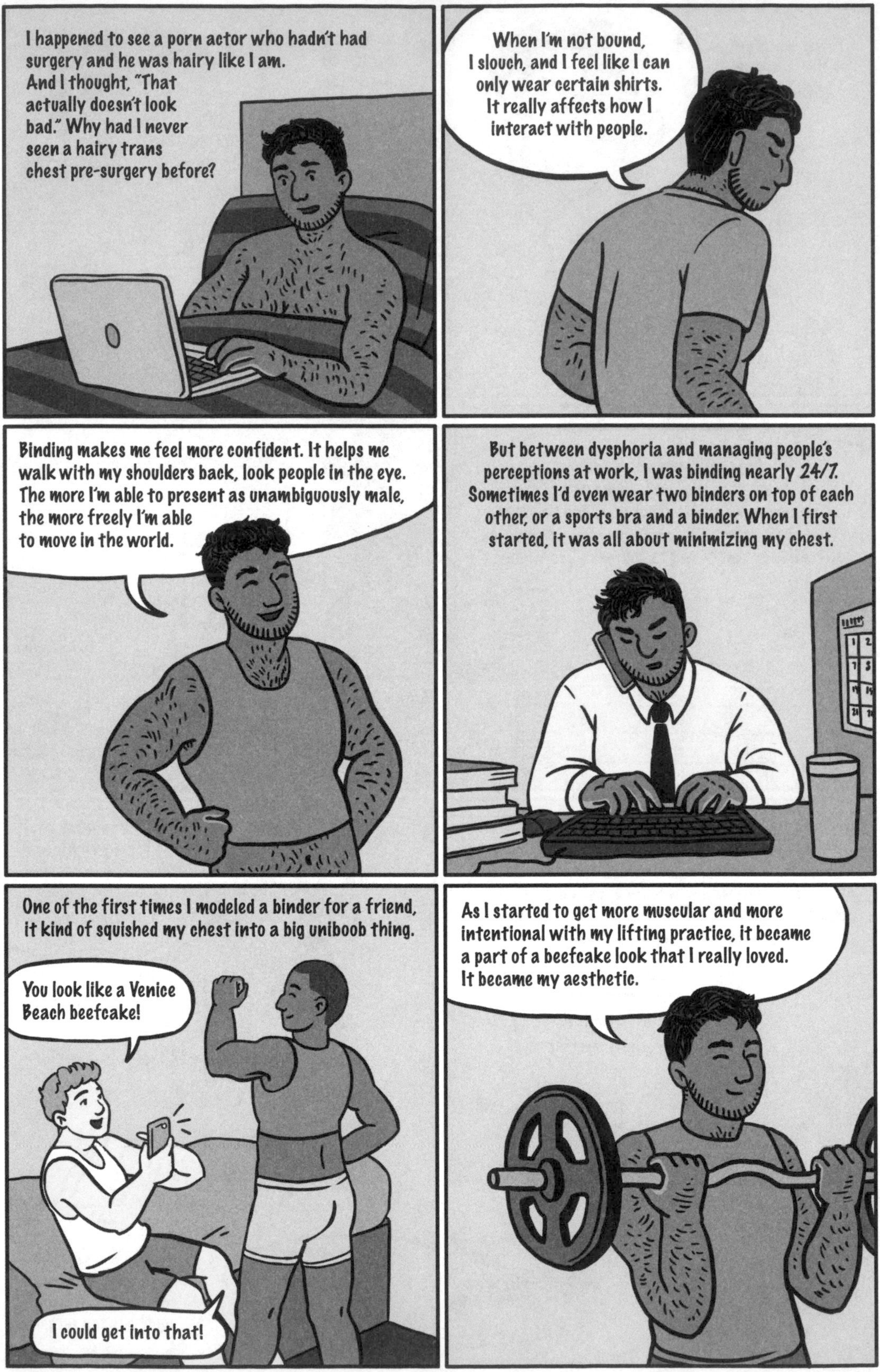
I happened to see a porn actor who hadn't had surgery and he was hairy like I am. And I thought, "That actually doesn't look bad." Why had I never seen a hairy trans chest pre-surgery before?
When I'm not bound, I slouch, and I feel like I can only wear certain shirts. It really affects how I interact with people.
Binding makes me feel more confident. It helps me walk with my shoulders back, look people in the eye. The more I'm able to present as unambiguously male, the more freely I'm able to move in the world.
But between dysphoria and managing people's perceptions at work, I was binding nearly 24/7. Sometimes I'd even wear two binders on top of each other, or a sports bra and a binder. When I first started, it was all about minimizing my chest.
One of the first times I modeled a binder for a friend, it kind of squished my chest into a big uniboob thing.
You look like a Venice Beach beefcake!
I could get into that!
As I started to get more muscular and more intentional with my lifting practice, it became a part of a beefcake look that I really loved. It became my aesthetic.

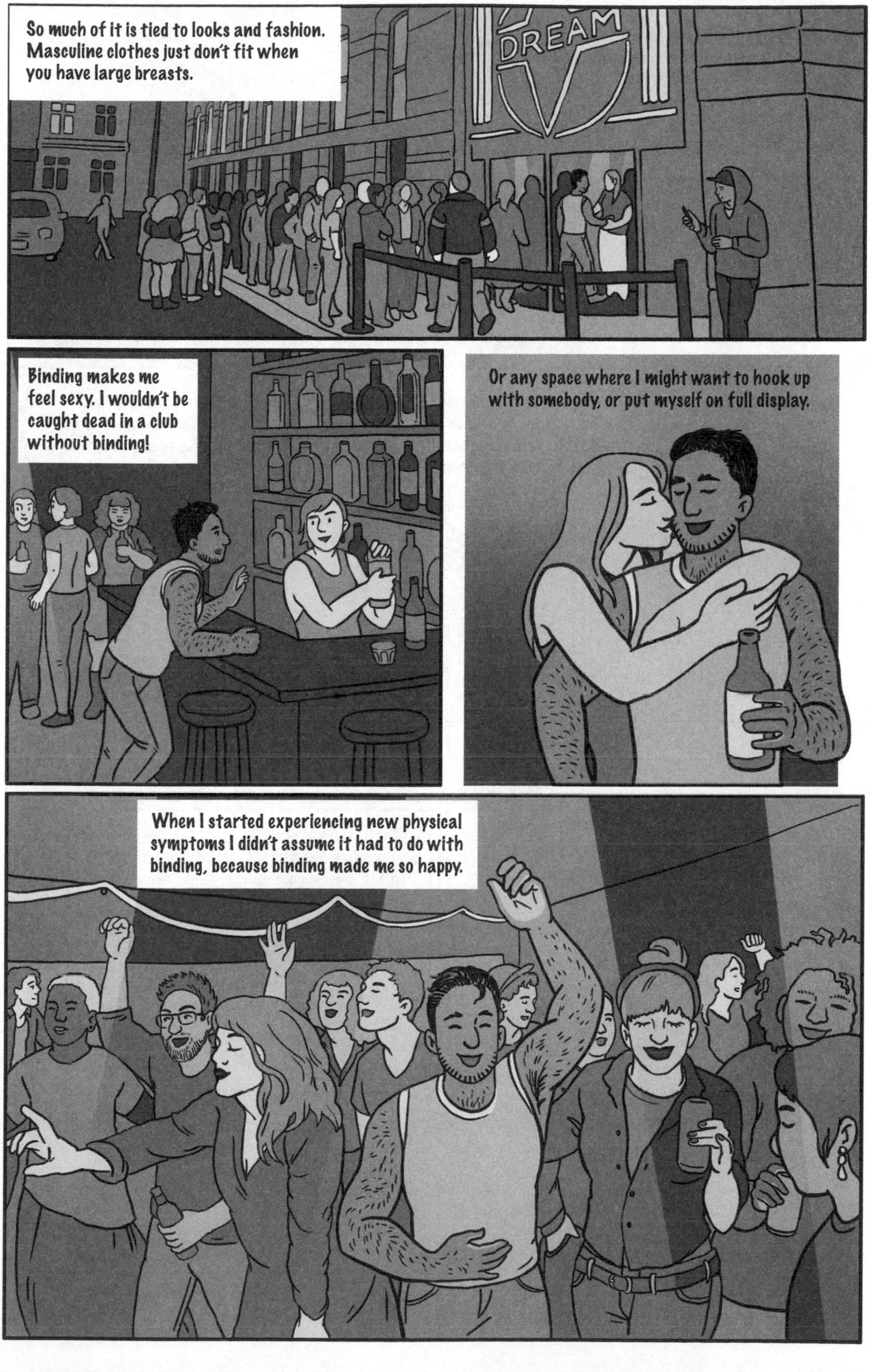
So much of it is tied to looks and fashion. Masculine clothes just don't fit when you have large breasts.
DREAM
Binding makes me feel sexy. I wouldn't be caught dead in a club without binding!
Or any space where I might want to hook up with somebody, or put myself on full display.
When I started experiencing new physical symptoms I didn't assume it had to do with binding, because binding made me so happy.

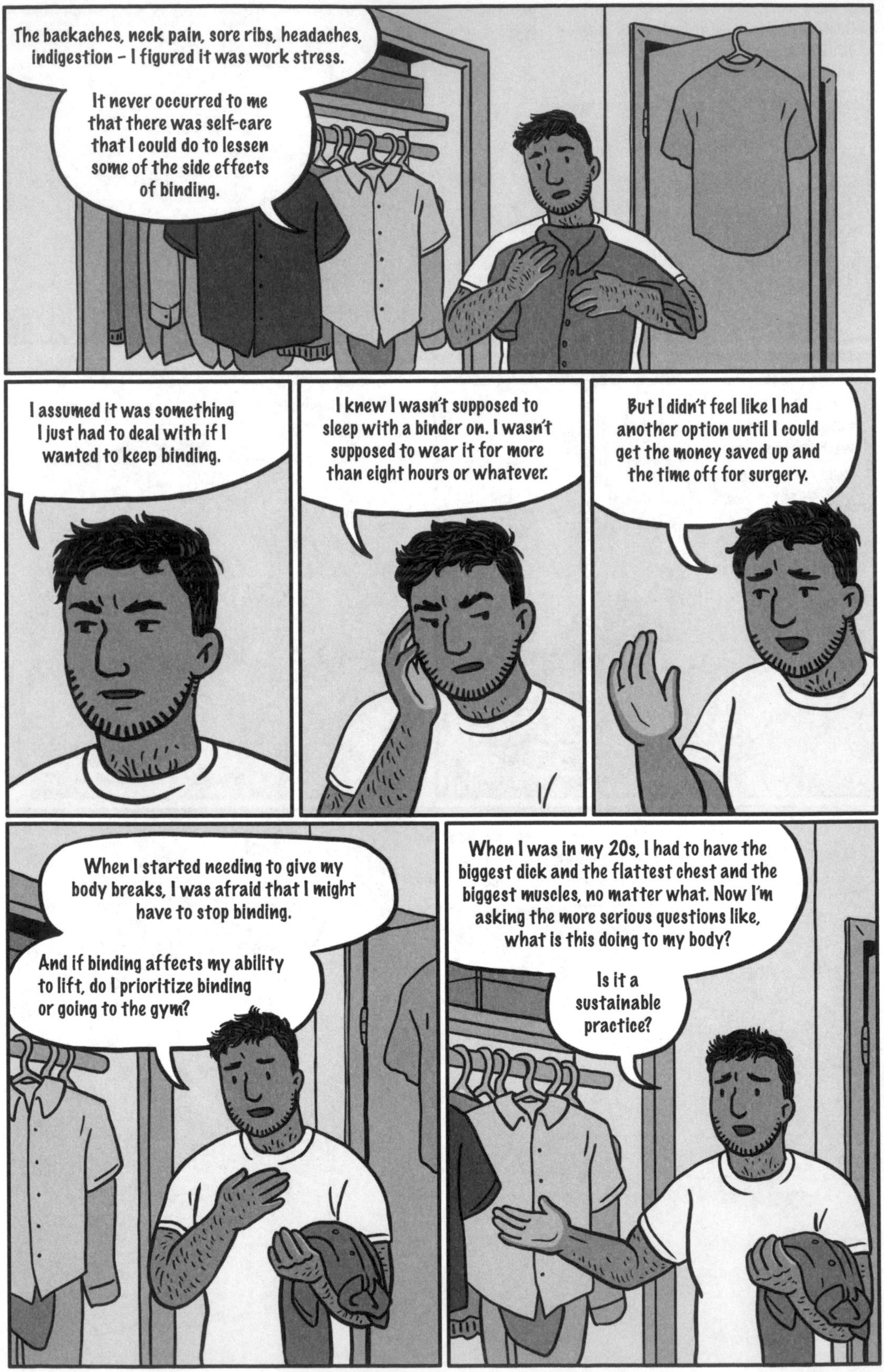
The backaches, neck pain, sore ribs, headaches, indigestion – I figured it was work stress.
It never occurred to me that there was self-care that I could do to lessen some of the side effects of binding.
I assumed it was something I just had to deal with if I wanted to keep binding.
I knew I wasn't supposed to sleep with a binder on. I wasn't supposed to wear it for more than eight hours or whatever.
But I didn't feel like I had another option until I could get the money saved up and the time off for surgery.
When I started needing to give my body breaks, I was afraid that I might have to stop binding.
And if binding affects my ability to lift, do I prioritize binding or going to the gym?
When I was in my 20s, I had to have the biggest dick and the flattest chest and the biggest muscles, no matter what. Now I'm asking the more serious questions like, what is this doing to my body?
Is it a sustainable practice?

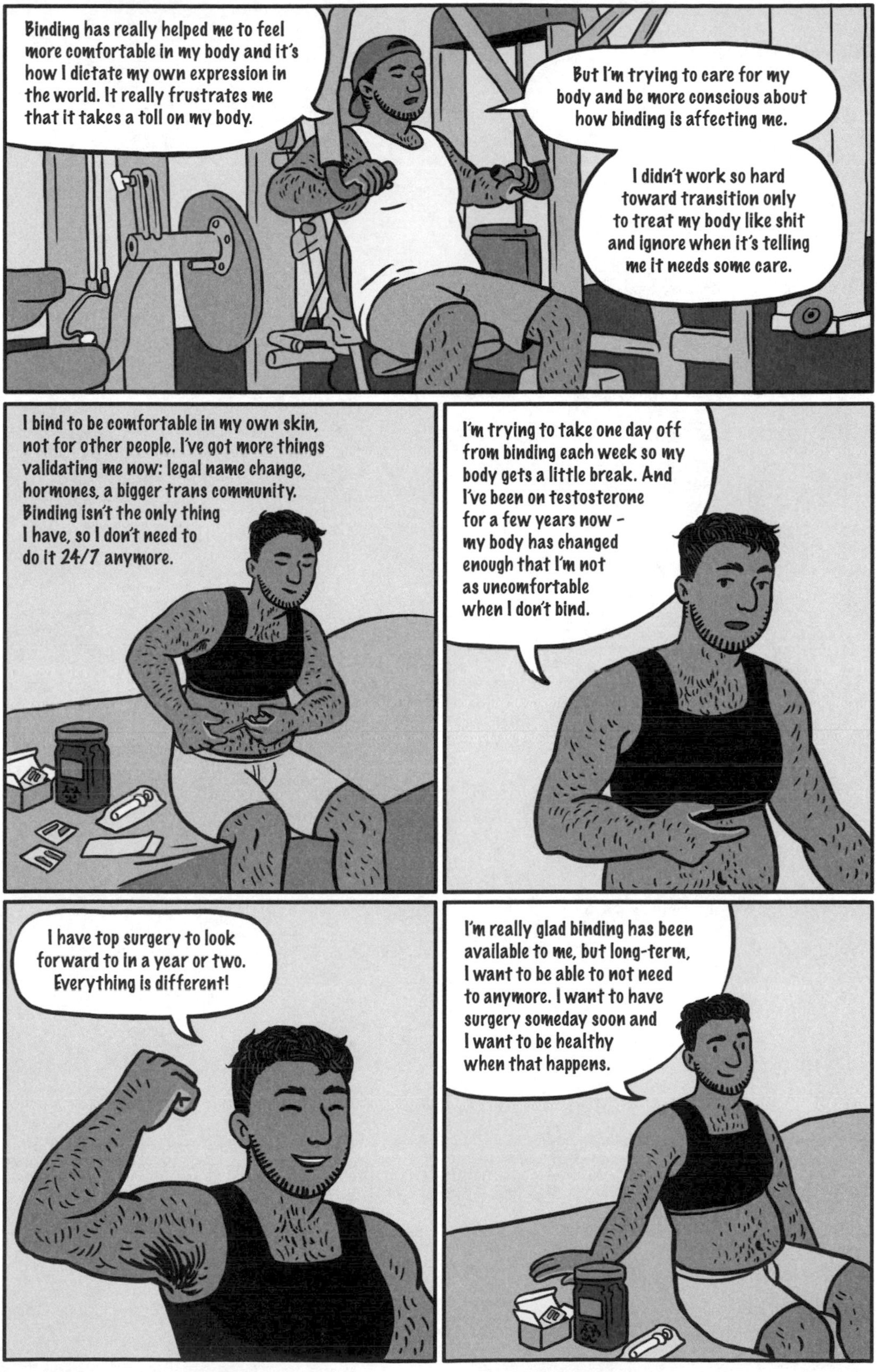
Binding has really helped me to feel more comfortable in my body and it's how I dictate my own expression in the world. It really frustrates me that it takes a toll on my body.
But I'm trying to care for my body and be more conscious about how binding is affecting me.
I didn't work so hard toward transition only to treat my body like shit and ignore when it's telling me it needs some care.
I bind to be comfortable in my own skin, not for other people. I've got more things validating me now: legal name change, hormones, a bigger trans community. Binding isn't the only thing I have, so I don't need to do it 24/7 anymore.
I'm trying to take one day off from binding each week so my body gets a little break. And I've been on testosterone for a few years now - my body has changed enough that I'm not as uncomfortable when I don't bind.
I have top surgery to look forward to in a year or two. Everything is different!
I'm really glad binding has been available to me, but long-term, I want to be able to not need to anymore. I want to have surgery someday soon and I want to be healthy when that happens.

C, 19 years old, he/they

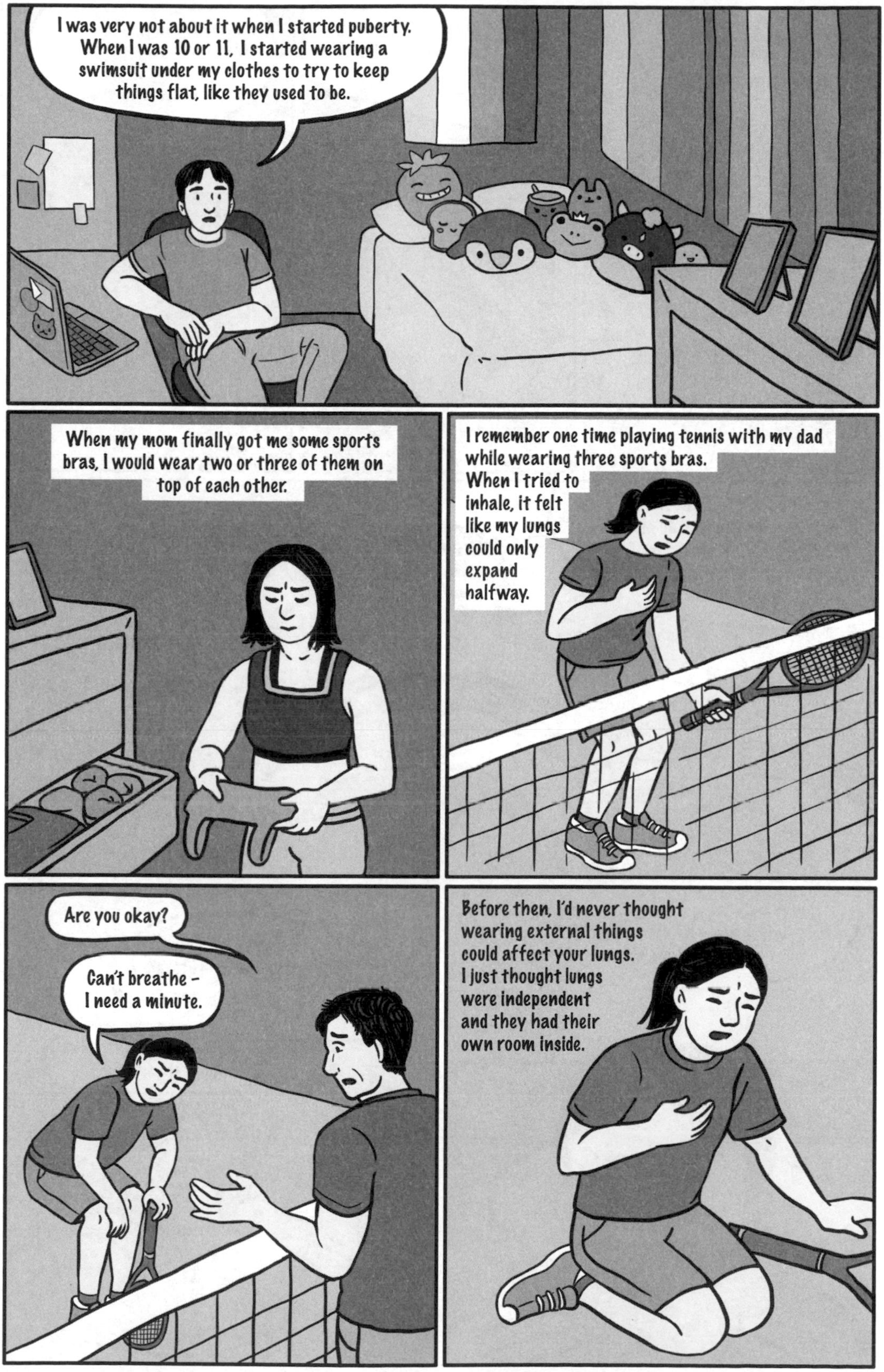
I was very not about it when I started puberty. When I was 10 or 11, I started wearing a swimsuit under my clothes to try to keep things flat, like they used to be.
When my mom finally got me some sports bras, I would wear two or three of them on top of each other.
I remember one time playing tennis with my dad while wearing three sports bras. When I tried to inhale, it felt like my lungs could only expand halfway.
Are you okay?
Can't breathe - I need a minute.
Before then, I'd never thought wearing external things could affect your lungs. I just thought lungs were independent and they had their own room inside.

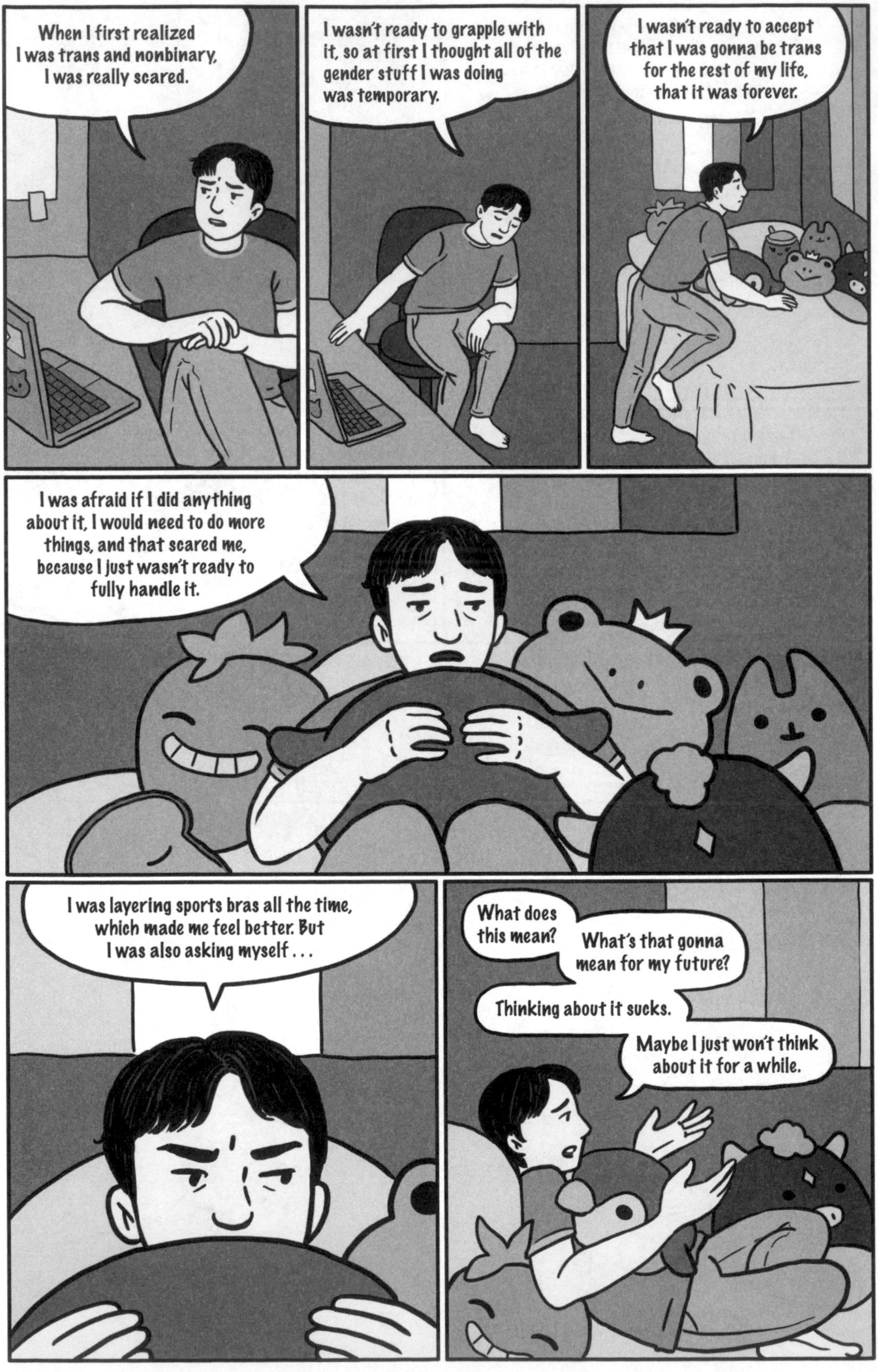
When I first realized I was trans and nonbinary, I was really scared.
I wasn't ready to grapple with it, so at first I thought all of the gender stuff I was doing was temporary.
I wasn't ready to accept that I was gonna be trans for the rest of my life, that it was forever.
I was afraid if I did anything about it, I would need to do more things, and that scared me, because I just wasn't ready to fully handle it.
I was layering sports bras all the time, which made me feel better. But I was also asking myself . . .
What does this mean?
What's that gonna mean for my future?
Thinking about it sucks.
Maybe I just won't think about it for a while.

So for a while I stopped. Stopped binding so I could stop asking myself those questions.

But then I also stopped eating, and started exercising a lot. At the time it seemed good, because I had less curves.

I was operating my body at a remove. I was not in my body. In order to function in the world there was a certain degree of dissociation that I just had as a baseline.

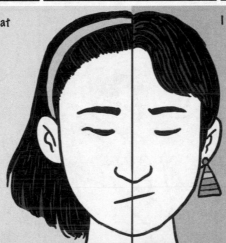

I had accepted the idea that I was supposed to be uncomfortable with my body. And that was okay, because my body was not really for me.

I feel like I've been unlearning that, from age 15 or 16 till now. And learning to own the space that I take up, and understand that it's my body, and it is for me. I'm gonna do what I want and what feels best. As opposed to just accepting the discomfort.

Eventually I accepted that it was a real thing. How I felt was valid. I started to be able to articulate that I wasn't comfortable with my body but I didn't really know what to do about it.

LGBTQ+

SURPASSING CERTAINTY
SPELL BOUND
THE THIRD PERSON
NONBINARY: MEMOIRS OF GENDER AND IDENTITY
SORTED
SISSY: a coming-of-gender story

FEMME IN PUBLIC
FUN HOME
OUT OF SALEM
A YEAR WITHOUT A NAME
GENDER QUEER

ACROSS A FIELD OF STARLIGHT
KISSES FOR JET
I HOPE WE CHOOSE LOVE
PANSY
SNAPDRAGON
SHE WANTS IT: Desire, Power, and Toppling the Patriarchy

In high school I learned about transgender identities and finally had words to describe dysphoria and identity. I learned that binders exist, and I ordered a real one.

GENDER QUEER
A MEMOIR

When it arrived, I tried to put it on and struggled.

I had to step into it and shimmy it up feet first. It took five sweaty minutes.

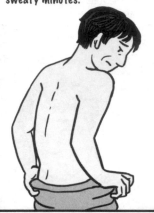

It was so tight that I could barely move or breathe.

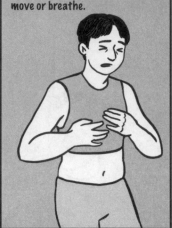

And I pulled something in my neck trying to get it off again.

!

My mom had to rescue me!

Ow!

This can't be right. Where did you get this? I'm ordering you a bigger size.

Waiting for the next size to come in the mail was the longest week of my life.

But then I put it on, and it actually looked better than the smaller size. And it didn't leave red marks on my skin.

The level of excitement I had around the binder . . . It helped me be more sure of myself. If something brings you that much happiness, you should listen to it!

I also started trying trans tape. I went to the beach with my friends over the summer and I wore the tape into the ocean.

Binding makes my body feel more like my own. It affects how I want to take care of myself.

It eased a lot of my anxiety and depression, it helped me climb back out of an eating disorder.

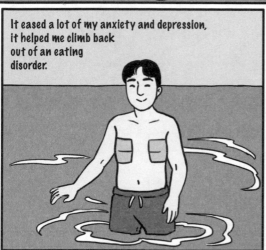

Binding gave me the freedom to exist.

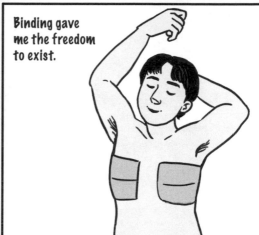

I've considered taking hormones. But I don't think I'm ready for that...

Without society's perception of me as female, I wouldn't even be thinking about hormones. But even if I was totally in isolation... I'd still be binding.

Binding is something I do for myself.

D, 56 years old, they/them

I grew up in the seventies and couldn't disclose who I was at home. So I'd leave the house in dresses and tights, because that's what my mom wanted me to wear. I'd hide behind the bushes at the bus stop, and change into a T-shirt and jeans before school.

I had a kind of binder top that I'd made myself, by cutting the legs off some control-top pantyhose and just keeping the top elastic part. I had to hand wash it and hang it up to dry, and I didn't want my mom to see it, so I had to be sneaky.

I was always nervous about it ... I'd heard stories about people like me getting beat up. I wasn't out to anyone, so my binder was the only thing that might give me away. But even that fear was worth it, because of how glorious it felt seeing myself in the mirror in the right clothes.

It was pretty rare that I would actually wear it, just 'cause I was afraid if I wore it too often, people would notice. Would my parents notice?

Freshman year of high school, my mom found my binder. She freaked, and she burned it on the porch.

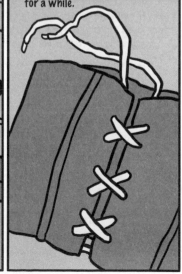

So I made a new binder out of some jeans and shoelaces that actually worked pretty well for a while.

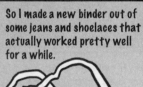

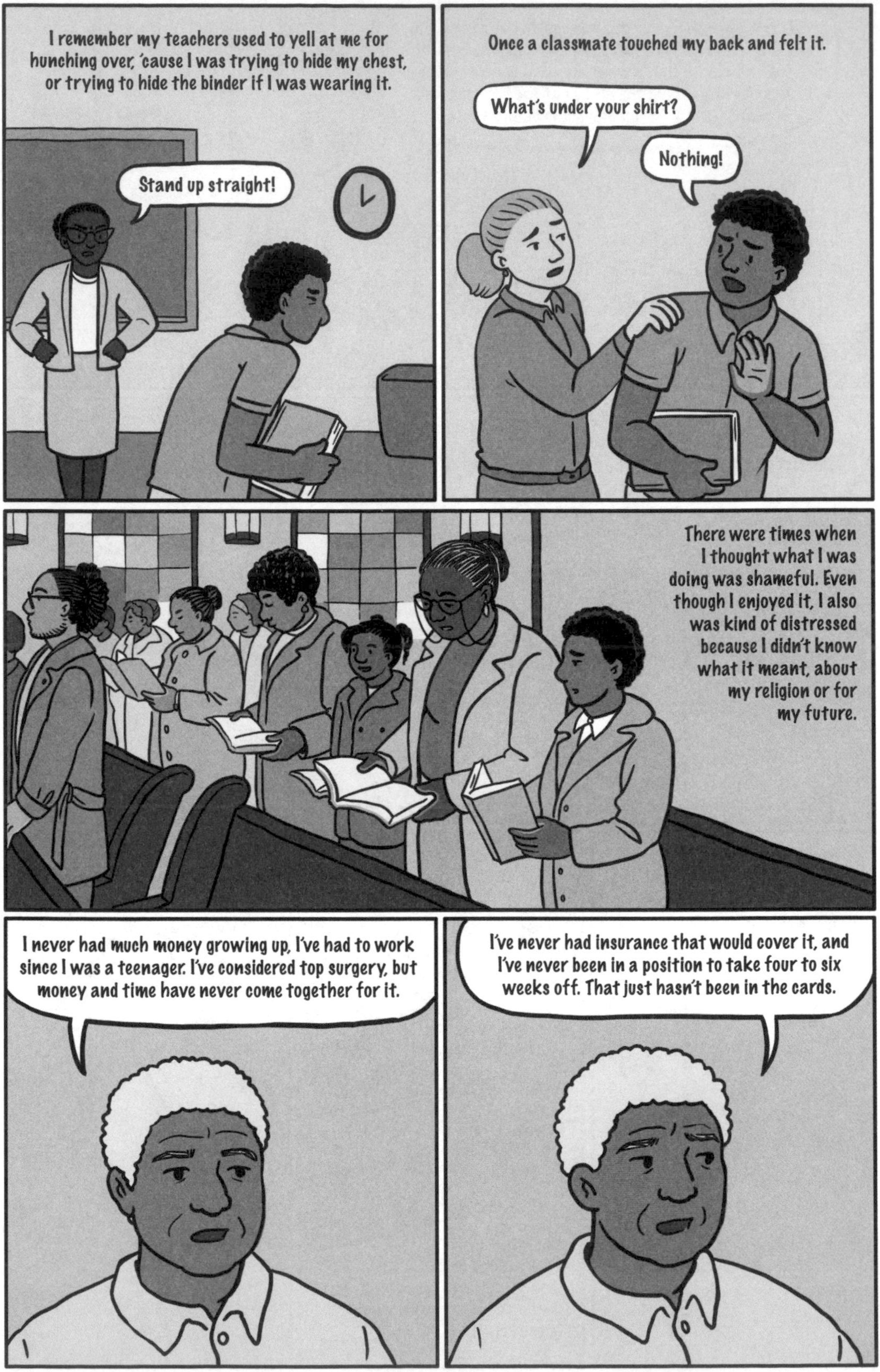
I remember my teachers used to yell at me for hunching over, 'cause I was trying to hide my chest, or trying to hide the binder if I was wearing it.
Stand up straight!
Once a classmate touched my back and felt it.
What's under your shirt?
Nothing!
There were times when I thought what I was doing was shameful. Even though I enjoyed it, I also was kind of distressed because I didn't know what it meant, about my religion or for my future.
I never had much money growing up, I've had to work since I was a teenager. I've considered top surgery, but money and time have never come together for it.
I've never had insurance that would cover it, and I've never been in a position to take four to six weeks off. That just hasn't been in the cards.

When I moved out of the house, I would do a small sports bra and then a homemade binder.

Or I would use elastic bandages, but I quickly realized those had serious bad health effects! Including compressing my lungs so badly I couldn't breathe even after I took them off.

The ACE bandages cut into my skin and I got this rattling sound in my lungs.

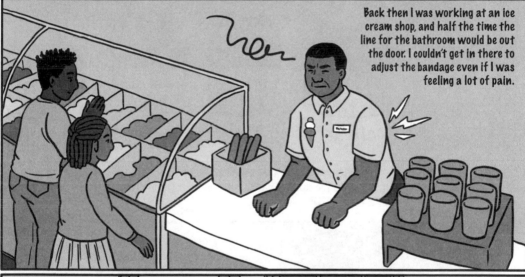

Back then I was working at an ice cream shop, and half the time the line for the bathroom would be out the door. I couldn't get in there to adjust the bandage even if I was feeling a lot of pain.

I've always bound at work, to try and avoid being misgendered, but binding for long shifts can be tough on my body.

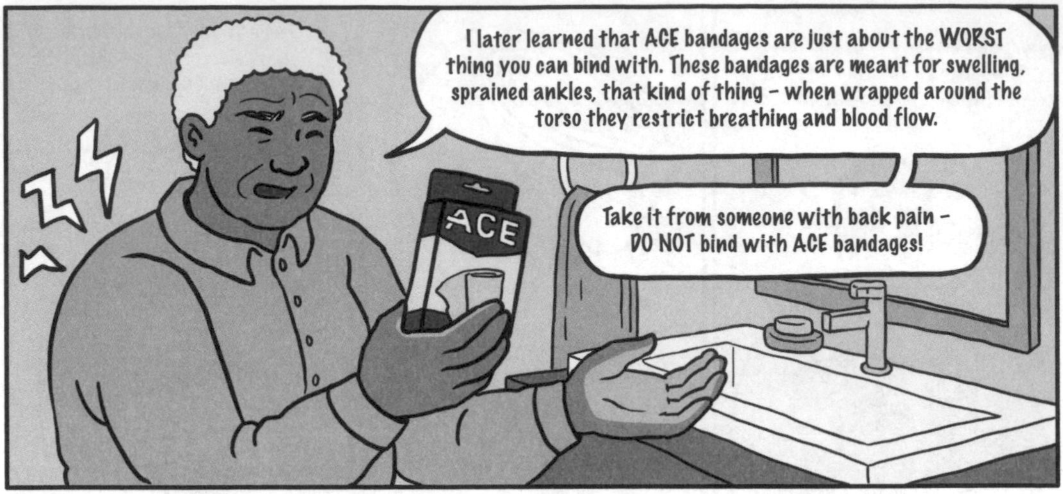
I later learned that ACE bandages are just about the WORST thing you can bind with. These bandages are meant for swelling, sprained ankles, that kind of thing – when wrapped around the torso they restrict breathing and blood flow.
ACE
Take it from someone with back pain – DO NOT bind with ACE bandages!

The binders available now are SO MUCH better than what I could get in my 20s and 30s!

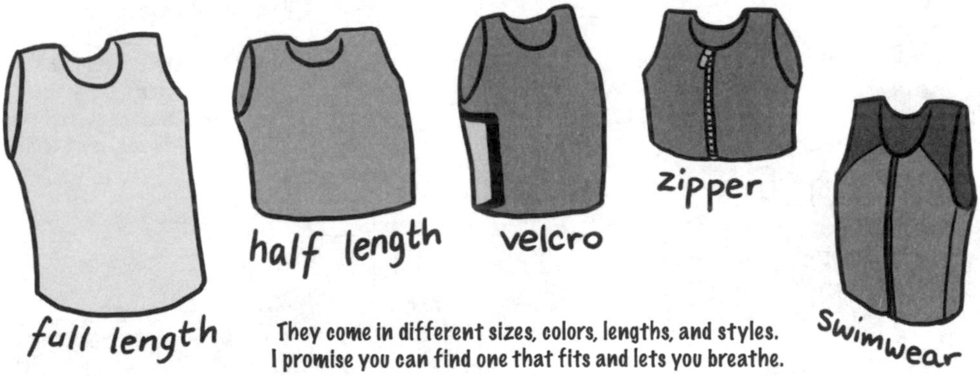
full length
half length
velcro
zipper
swimwear

They come in different sizes, colors, lengths, and styles.
I promise you can find one that fits and lets you breathe.

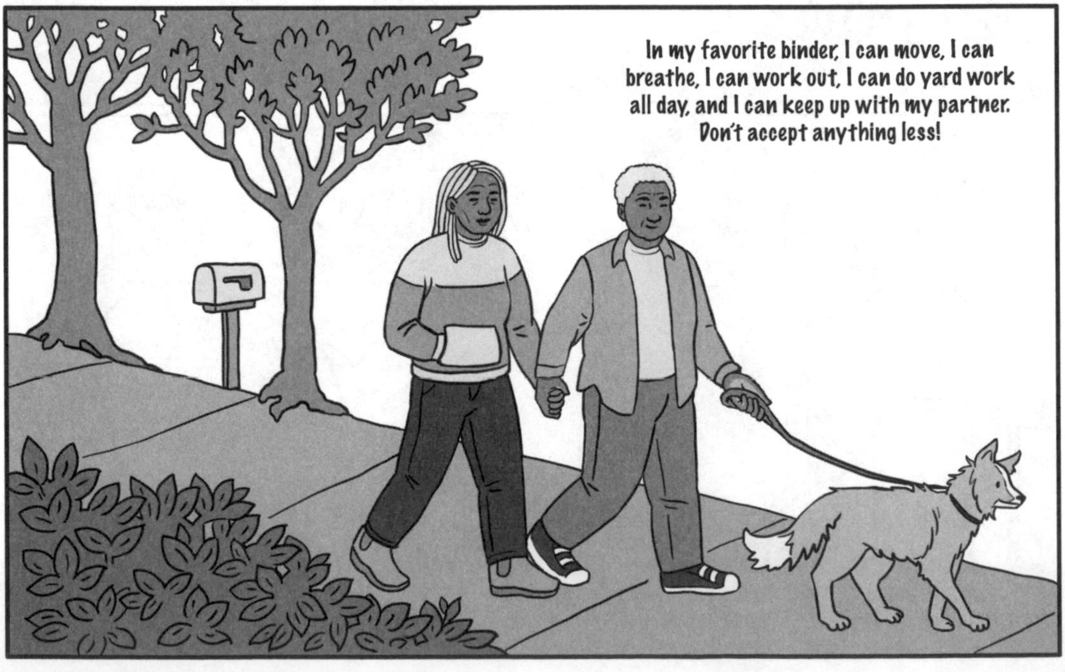
In my favorite binder, I can move, I can breathe, I can work out, I can do yard work all day, and I can keep up with my partner. Don't accept anything less!

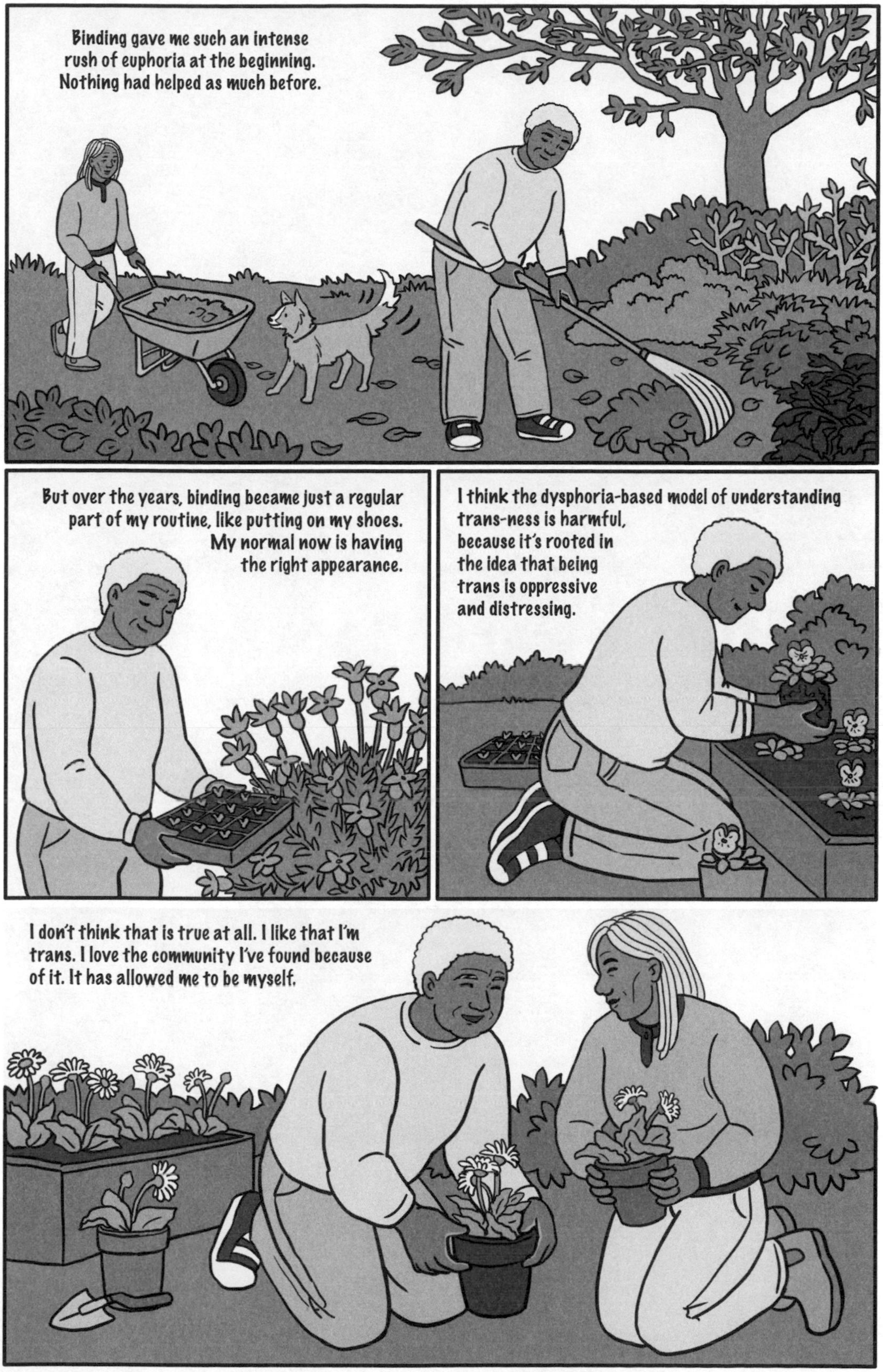
Binding gave me such an intense rush of euphoria at the beginning. Nothing had helped as much before.
But over the years, binding became just a regular part of my routine, like putting on my shoes. My normal now is having the right appearance.
I think the dysphoria-based model of understanding trans-ness is harmful, because it's rooted in the idea that being trans is oppressive and distressing.
I don't think that is true at all. I like that I'm trans. I love the community I've found because of it. It has allowed me to be myself.

Tips & Tools for Healthy Binding

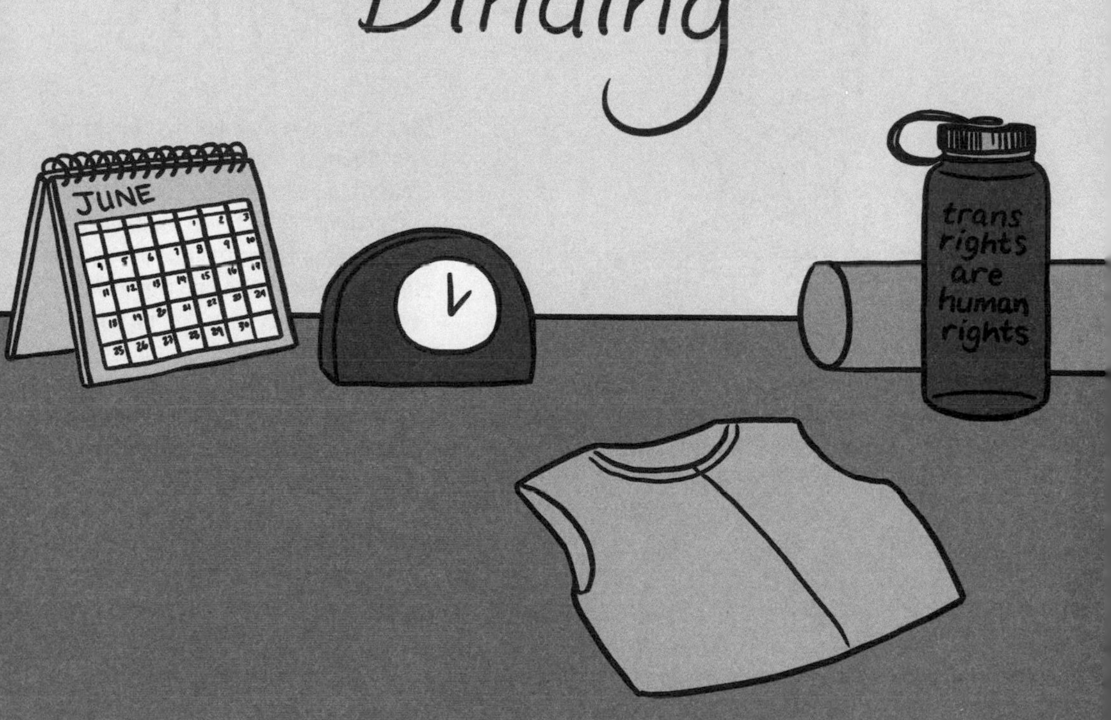
JUNE
trans rights are human rights

Binding your chest can affect many areas of your body. Most obviously, it can irritate your skin, but it can also affect the structures beneath the skin: your spine, ribs, and lungs.

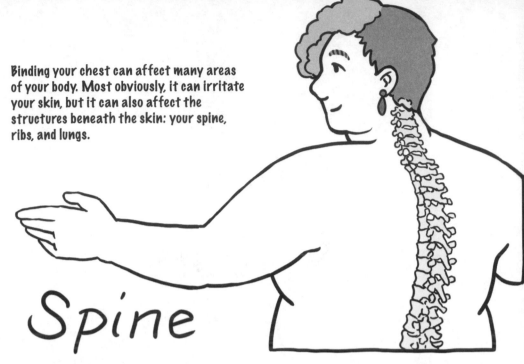

Spine

Your spine is a column of vertebrae connected by ligaments and muscles. When you wear a binder, it restricts the movement in your upper back. The ligaments and muscles under the binder can become tight, short, and weak, while the areas above and below have to move more to compensate, all of which can cause stiffness and pain.

Ribs

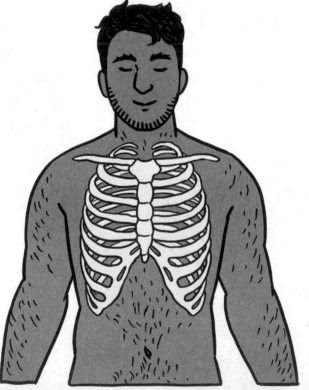

Your ribs have ligaments connecting them to your spine in the back, cartilage connecting them to your sternum in the front, and muscles connecting them to each other. The ribs are designed to move out and up when we breathe in. When you are wearing a binder, your ribs are compressed. The ligaments and muscles can tighten and shorten over time, decreasing your lung capacity even when not wearing the binder. Their connections to your spine stiffen up, forcing the connections to your sternum to move more than they should to breathe. This can cause sharp pain by the sternum, or occasionally rib fractures.

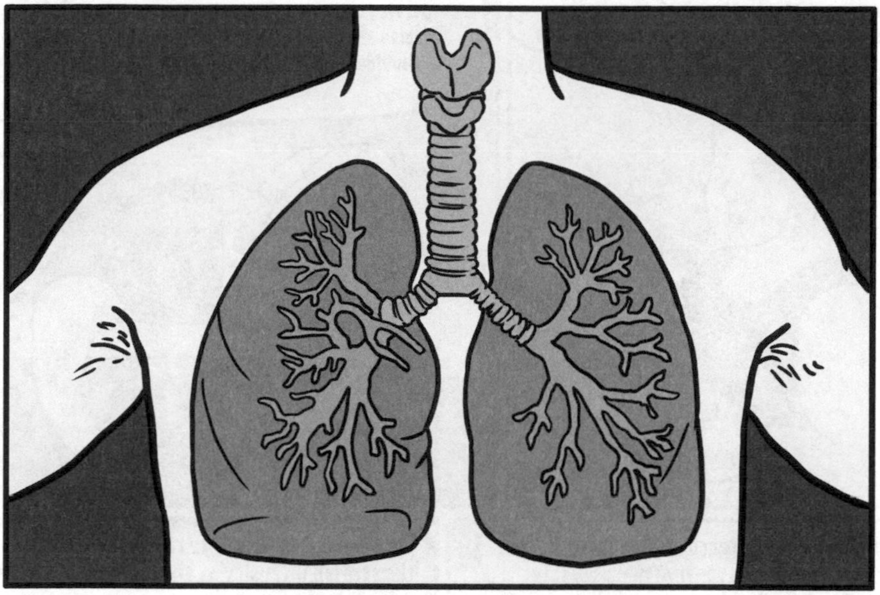

Lungs

Your lungs are a self-cleaning organ that needs a consistent flow of clean air to stay healthy. When you wear a binder, your lungs are restricted, especially around the widest part. In order to breathe, you have to expand more through the upper parts of your lungs, which are much smaller. This makes it harder to get oxygen and can make you lightheaded. The parts of your lungs that stay closed can become sticky, develop mucus, and breed bacteria, sometimes causing a chronic cough or pneumonia.

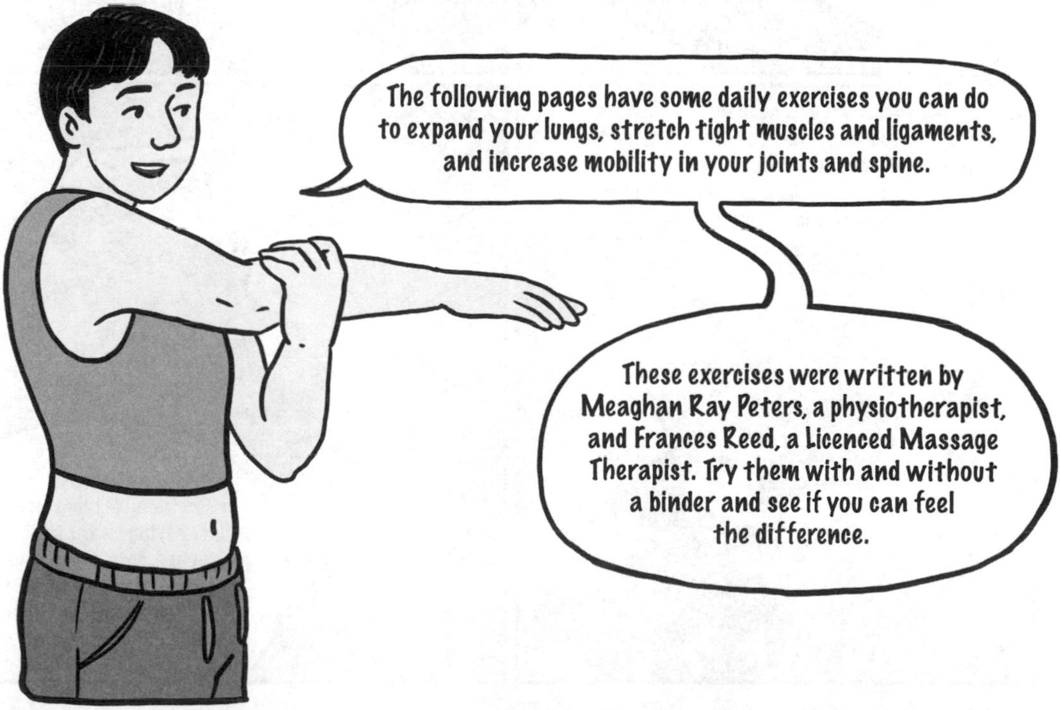
The following pages have some daily exercises you can do to expand your lungs, stretch tight muscles and ligaments, and increase mobility in your joints and spine.
These exercises were written by Meaghan Ray Peters, a physiotherapist, and Frances Reed, a Licenced Massage Therapist. Try them with and without a binder and see if you can feel the difference.

This chest opener will help release tightness in the upper chest and the front of the shoulder. You'll need a foam roller or a rolled up yoga mat.

Lay lengthwise on a rolled prop with your head and pelvis supported. Spread your arms in a T-shape. This exercise shouldn't be painful. If you experience pain in the shoulder, chest, or upper arms, support your elbows with blocks, books, or pillows.

Support

Support

You should feel a stretch across your chest, at the shoulder joint, and in the upper arm muscles. For three minutes, take deep breaths and allow gravity to pull your upper arms towards the floor.

Now bend your elbows to right angles. You should feel the stretch intensify at the front of your shoulders and along the front of your armpit. It's fine if your hands don't touch the floor, just take deep breaths for three minutes.

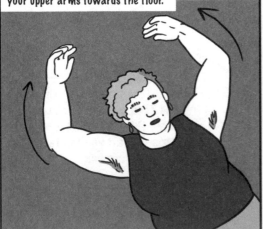

Next, bring your arms overhead with a slight bend in your elbows. You should feel the stretch along the back of your armpits and your upper arms. For about three minutes, take deep breaths and allow gravity to pull your upper arms towards the floor.

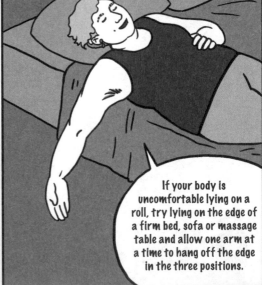

If your body is uncomfortable lying on a roll, try lying on the edge of a firm bed, sofa or massage table and allow one arm at a time to hang off the edge in the three positions.

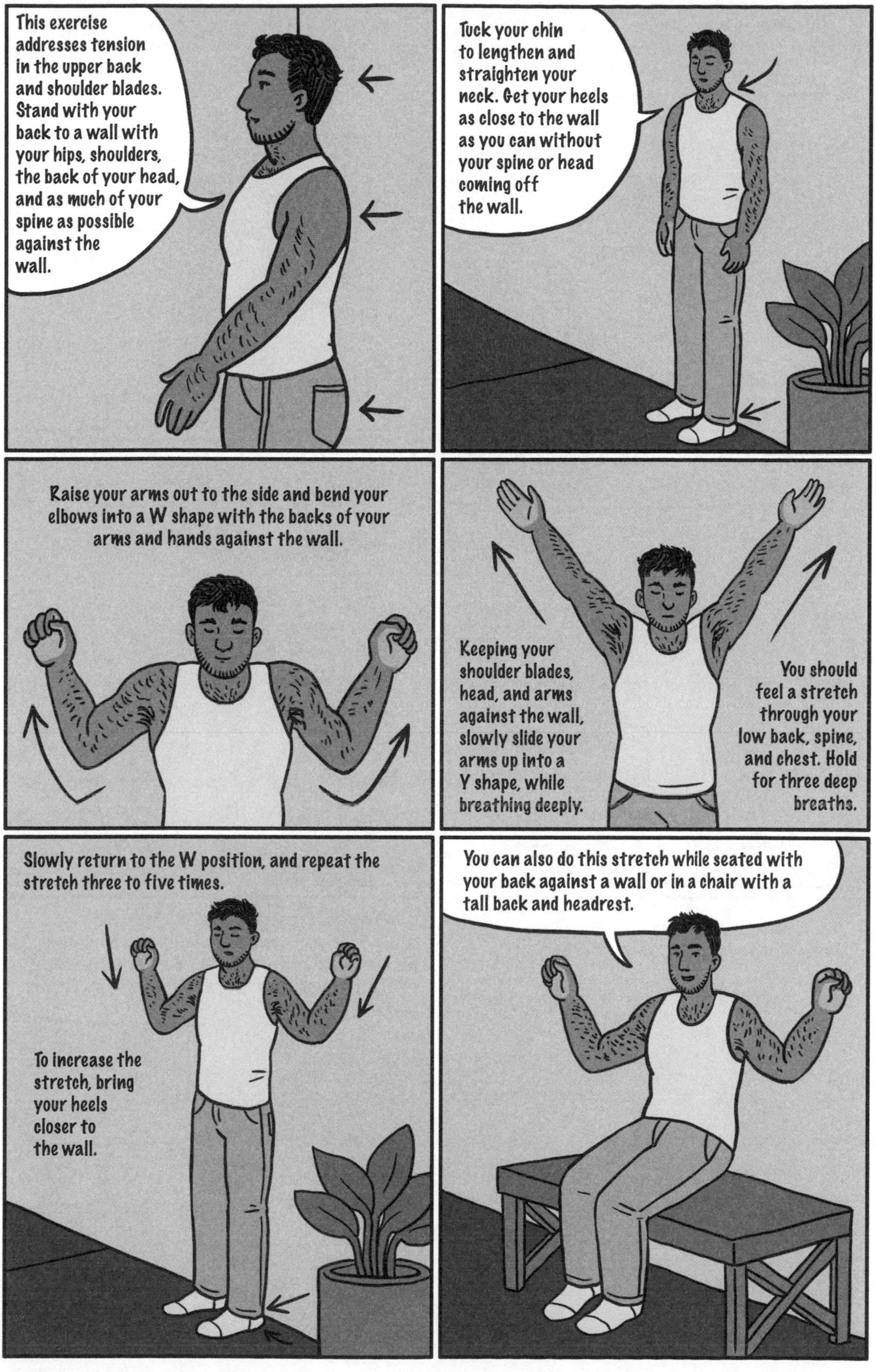
This exercise addresses tension in the upper back and shoulder blades. Stand with your back to a wall with your hips, shoulders, the back of your head, and as much of your spine as possible against the wall.
Tuck your chin to lengthen and straighten your neck. Get your heels as close to the wall as you can without your spine or head coming off the wall.
Raise your arms out to the side and bend your elbows into a W shape with the backs of your arms and hands against the wall.
Keeping your shoulder blades, head, and arms against the wall, slowly slide your arms up into a Y shape, while breathing deeply.
You should feel a stretch through your low back, spine, and chest. Hold for three deep breaths.
Slowly return to the W position, and repeat the stretch three to five times.
To increase the stretch, bring your heels closer to the wall.
You can also do this stretch while seated with your back against a wall or in a chair with a tall back and headrest.

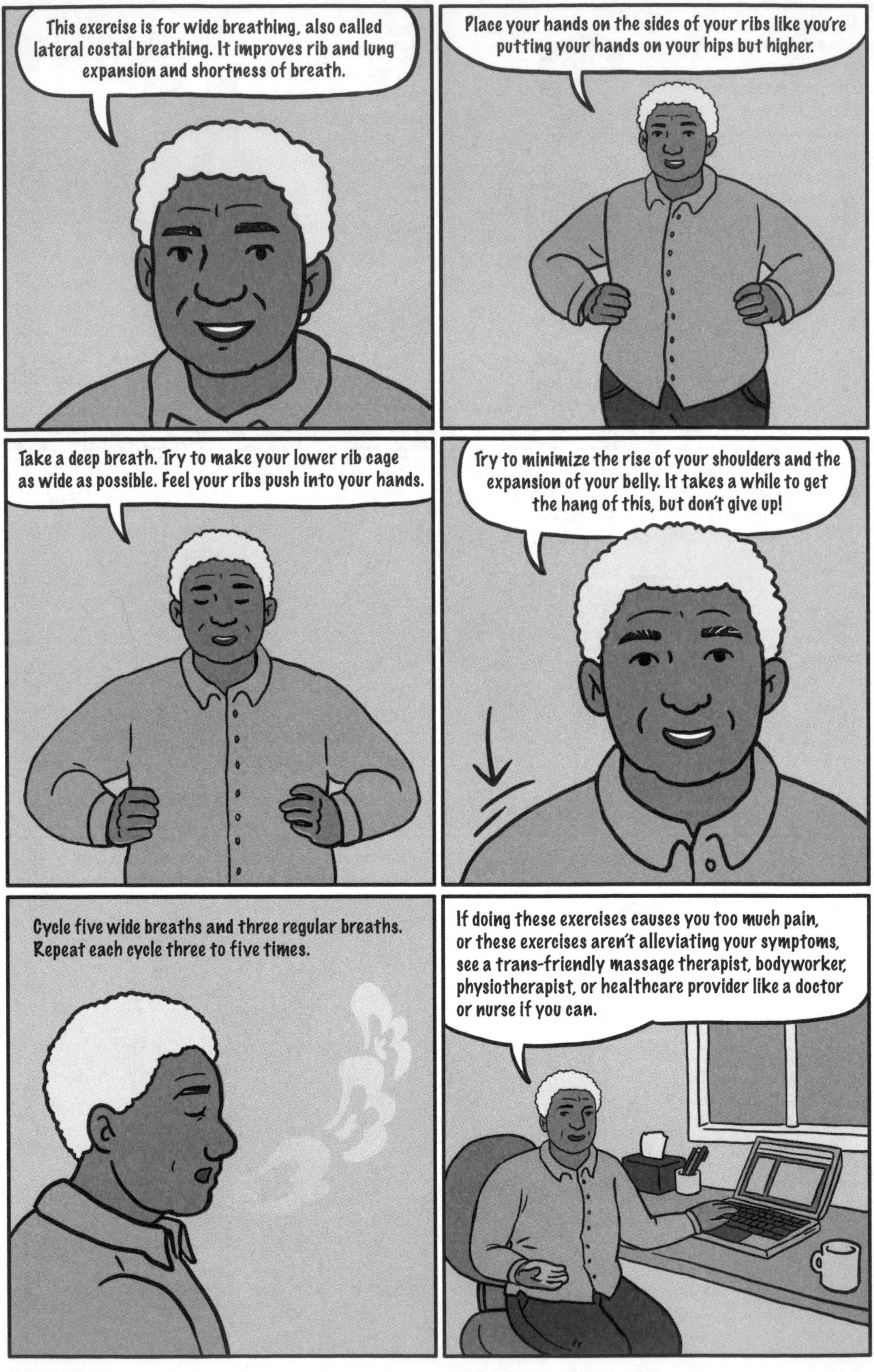
This exercise is for wide breathing, also called lateral costal breathing. It improves rib and lung expansion and shortness of breath.
Place your hands on the sides of your ribs like you're putting your hands on your hips but higher.
Take a deep breath. Try to make your lower rib cage as wide as possible. Feel your ribs push into your hands.
Try to minimize the rise of your shoulders and the expansion of your belly. It takes a while to get the hang of this, but don't give up!
Cycle five wide breaths and three regular breaths. Repeat each cycle three to five times.
If doing these exercises causes you too much pain, or these exercises aren't alleviating your symptoms, see a trans-friendly massage therapist, bodyworker, physiotherapist, or healthcare provider like a doctor or nurse if you can.

This exercise is for side bending and rotation of the upper spine. It improves rib and spine mobility and helps with chest pain, back pain, and shortness of breath.

While sitting in a sturdy chair, press one hand on your side.

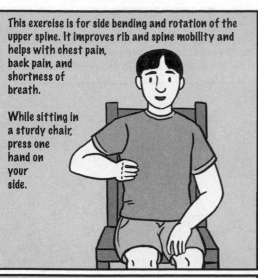

Place your open palm flat on your rib cage as high as you can comfortably go. Use this hand to apply firm pressure to your rib cage. This is your pivot point for the stretch.

Elbow at a Sharp angle

press side ribs →

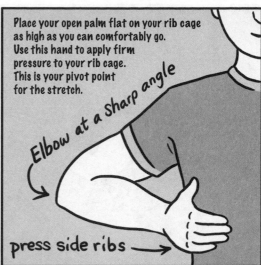

Reach the other arm up, then over, until you feel a stretch. Keep both butt cheeks pressed firmly into the chair.

Raised arm pressed to your ear

Weight evenly balanced on both legs →

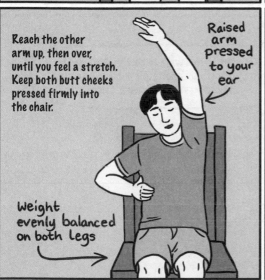

Hold for 10 to 20 seconds while taking deep breaths into your ribs like you did in the previous exercise.

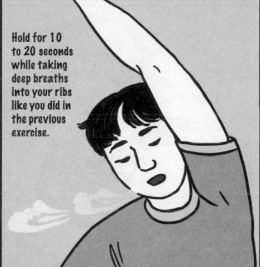

Then reach a little farther by twisting forward. Hold for 10 to 20 seconds while taking deep breaths.

Reach forward instead of directly upward

Repeat on the other side. Repeat both sides two more times.

Feel the stretch along here

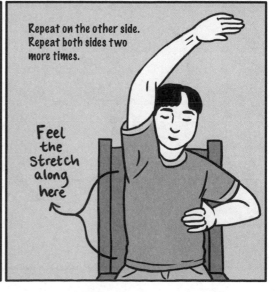

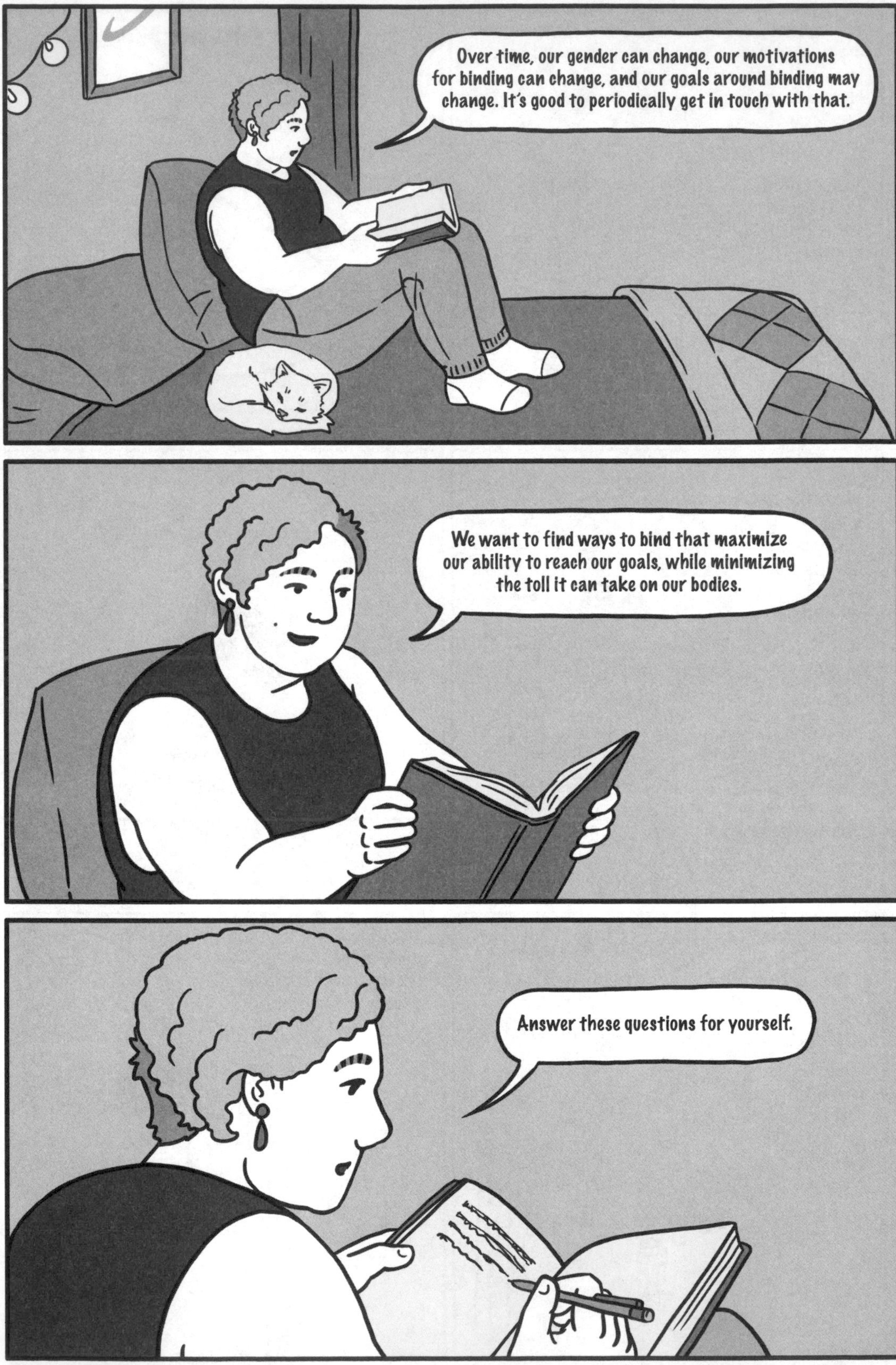
Over time, our gender can change, our motivations for binding can change, and our goals around binding may change. It's good to periodically get in touch with that.
We want to find ways to bind that maximize our ability to reach our goals, while minimizing the toll it can take on our bodies.
Answer these questions for yourself.

JOURNAL PROMPTS

What do I want my binding to do for me?

How do I want to look?

How does binding affect my mental health?

How does binding make me feel physically?

How does binding impact my ability to move safely in different spaces, if at all?

Can binding do everything I am hoping it will do?

Do I need to bring in additional ways to affirm my gender to reach my goals?

In what ways do I bind for myself and in what ways do I bind for other people?

How do I feel about this balance?

Are there other tools to affirm my gender or my safety that might reduce my need to bind?

CHECK IN WITH YOUR MOOD AND SYMPTOMS

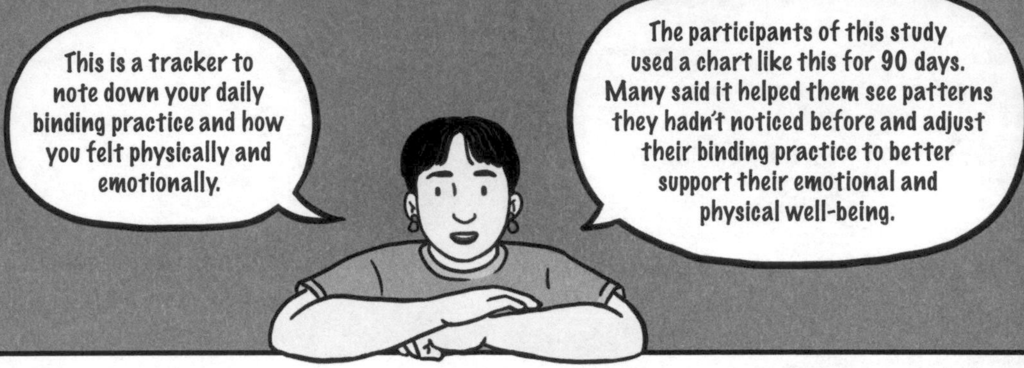
This is a tracker to note down your daily binding practice and how you felt physically and emotionally.
The participants of this study used a chart like this for 90 days. Many said it helped them see patterns they hadn't noticed before and adjust their binding practice to better support their emotional and physical well-being.

		MON	TUES	WED	THURS	FRI	SAT	SUN
HOW AM I FEELING EMOTIONALLY?	Feeling myself							
	Doing okay							
	Meh							
	Kinda blue							
	It's been rough							
HOW AM I FEELING PHYSICALLY?	Feeling comfy							
	Doing okay							
	Meh							
	Some pain							
	Pain all day							
HOW MANY HOURS DID I BIND?	0							
	2							
	4							
	6							
	8							
	10							
	12							
	14							
	16							
	18							
	20							
	22							
	24							

REFLECTION QUESTIONS

On the days I felt great in my body, what did that feel like?
What did I do that day to take care of myself? How can I do more of that?

On days that were tougher, either mentally or physically, what happened?
What helped me feel better afterward?

Is there a relationship between days where I feel good physically and mentally
and how long I wore my binder, or with what method of binding I used?

Is there a sweet spot for how long to bind to feel the best mentally and
physically?

How do I know when my body isn't responding well to binding?
What signs can I look out for?

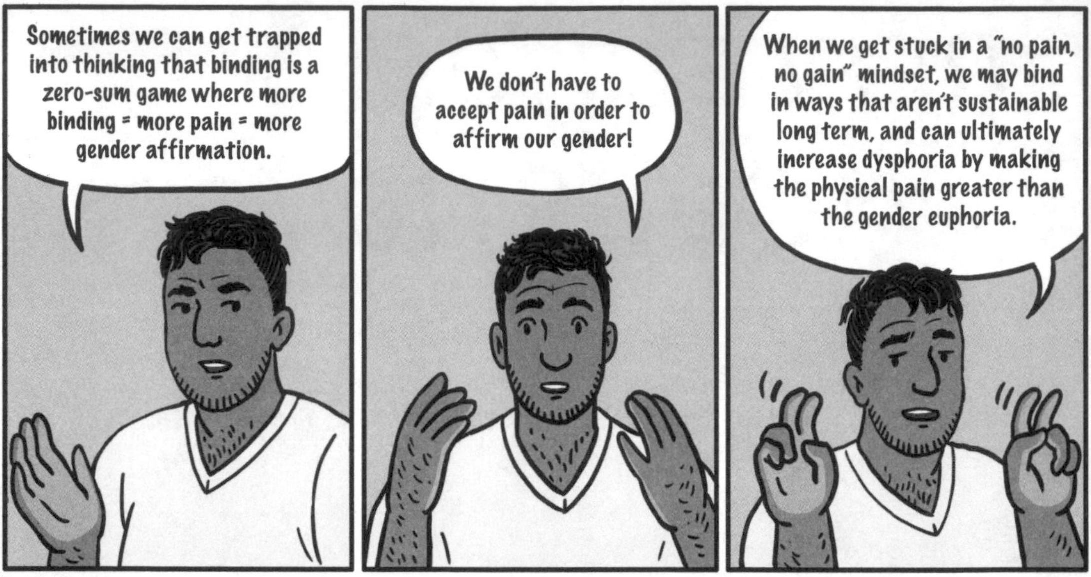
Sometimes we can get trapped into thinking that binding is a zero-sum game where more binding = more pain = more gender affirmation.
We don't have to accept pain in order to affirm our gender!
When we get stuck in a "no pain, no gain" mindset, we may bind in ways that aren't sustainable long term, and can ultimately increase dysphoria by making the physical pain greater than the gender euphoria.

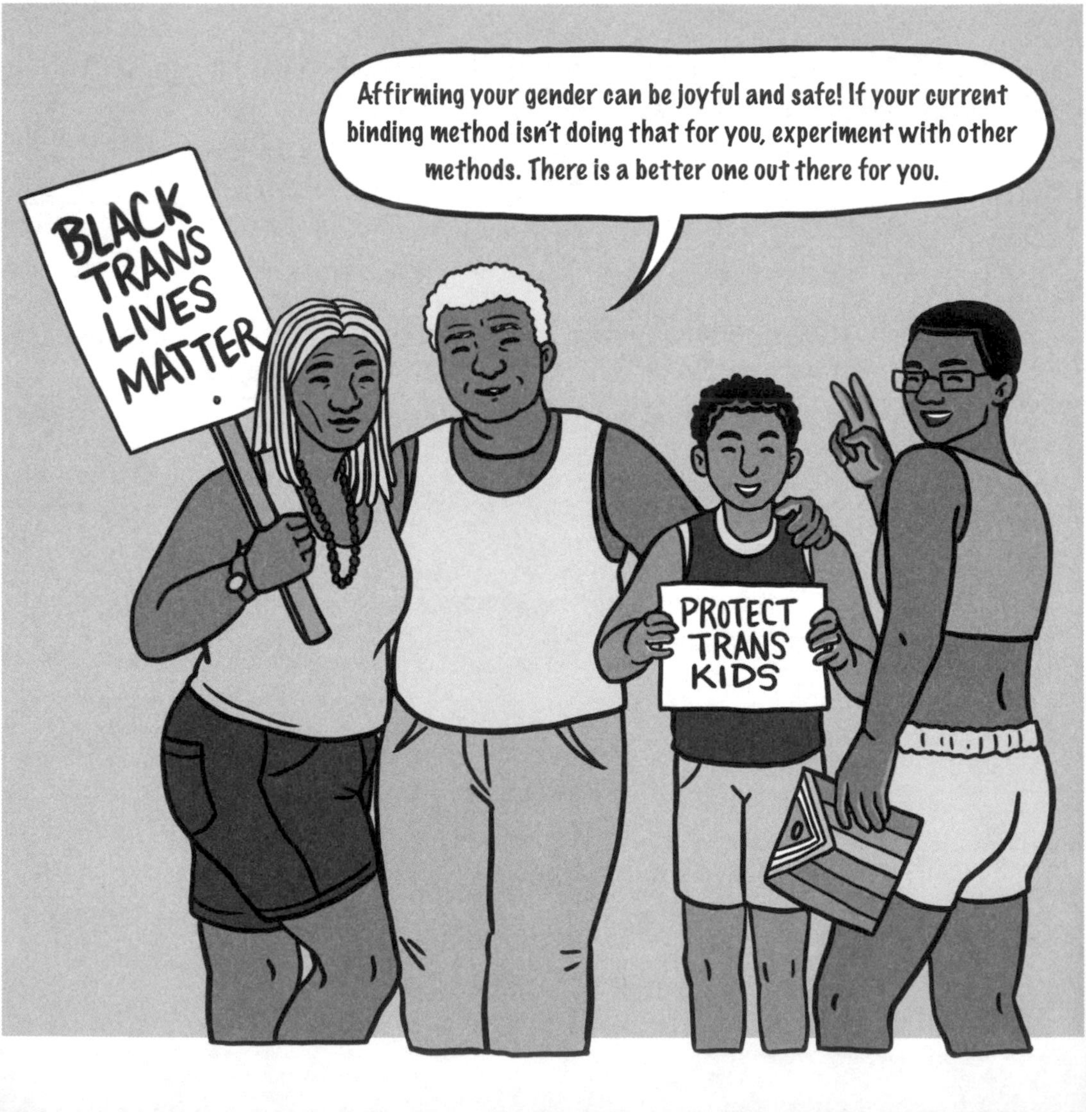
Affirming your gender can be joyful and safe! If your current binding method isn't doing that for you, experiment with other methods. There is a better one out there for you.
BLACK TRANS LIVES MATTER.
PROTECT TRANS KIDS

SOME STRATEGIES FOR REDUCING PAIN AND SIDE EFFECTS:

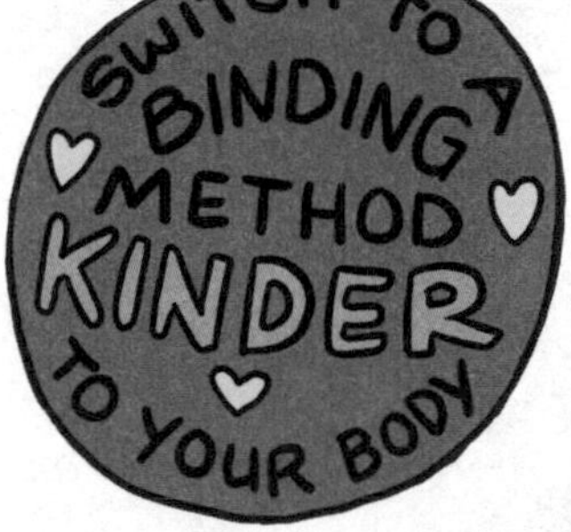
SWITCH TO A BINDING METHOD KINDER TO YOUR BODY

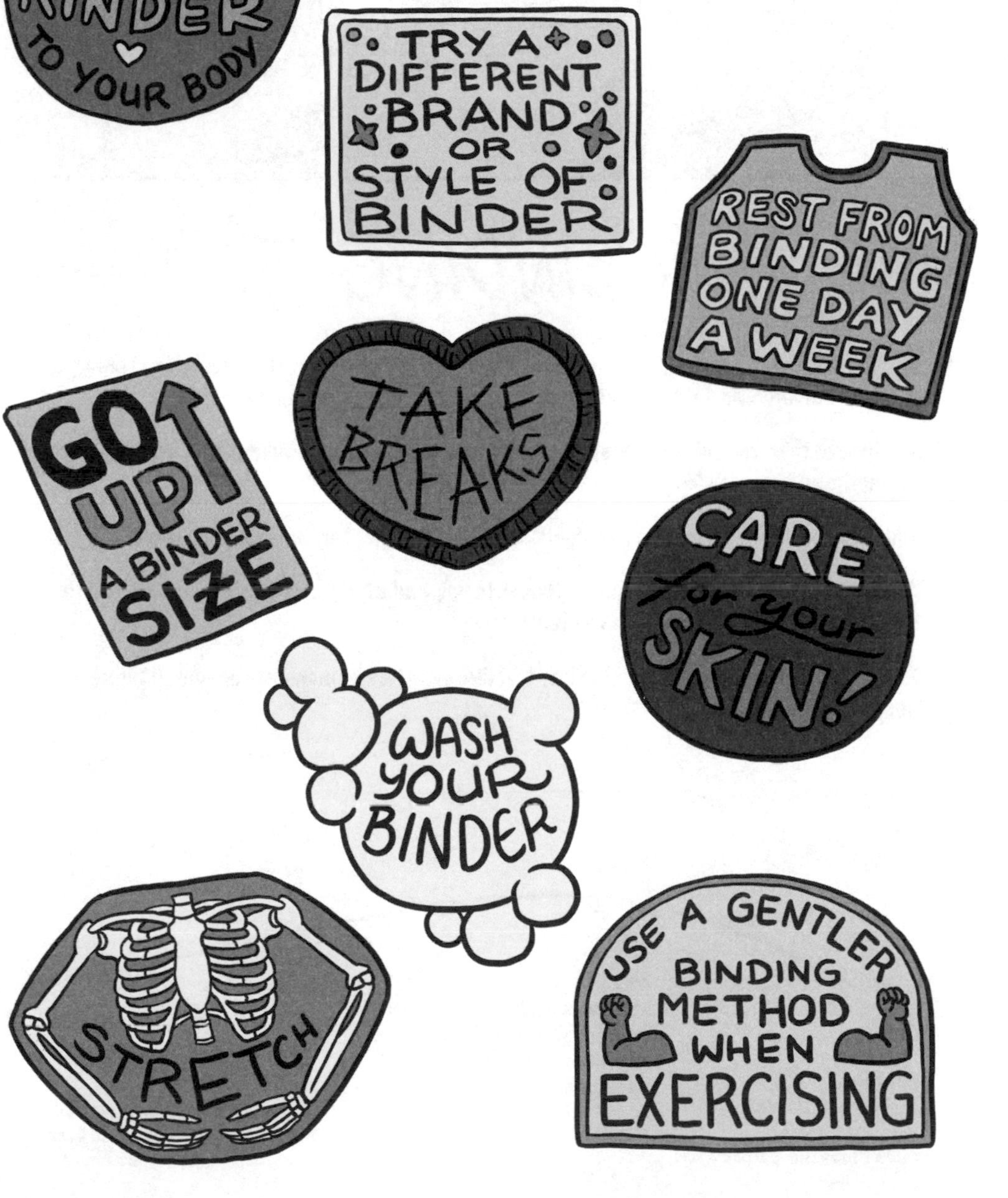
TRY A DIFFERENT BRAND OR STYLE OF BINDER
REST FROM BINDING ONE DAY A WEEK
GO UP A BINDER SIZE
TAKE BREAKS
CARE for your SKIN!
WASH YOUR BINDER
STRETCH
USE A GENTLER BINDING METHOD WHEN EXERCISING

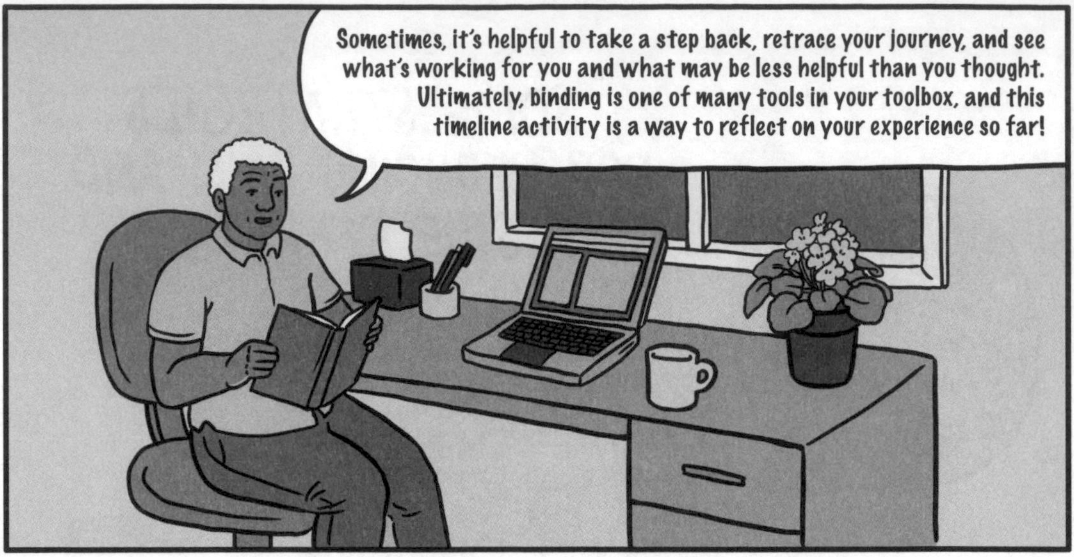
Sometimes, it's helpful to take a step back, retrace your journey, and see what's working for you and what may be less helpful than you thought. Ultimately, binding is one of many tools in your toolbox, and this timeline activity is a way to reflect on your experience so far!

MAP YOUR BINDING JOURNEY

- At the first circle, write the age when you first started binding. This can be anything you consider binding and does not necessarily have to include wearing an official binder.
- Add in whether you felt any symptoms at that time, and how binding made you feel about yourself and your gender.
- Add other moments that feel like significant changes to your binding experience.
- Reflect on the feelings, emotions, or thoughts you had at different points in your journey. Think about physical symptoms you felt.
- Continue to add in other moments that feel like significant moments on your binding journey.

Example from A's story

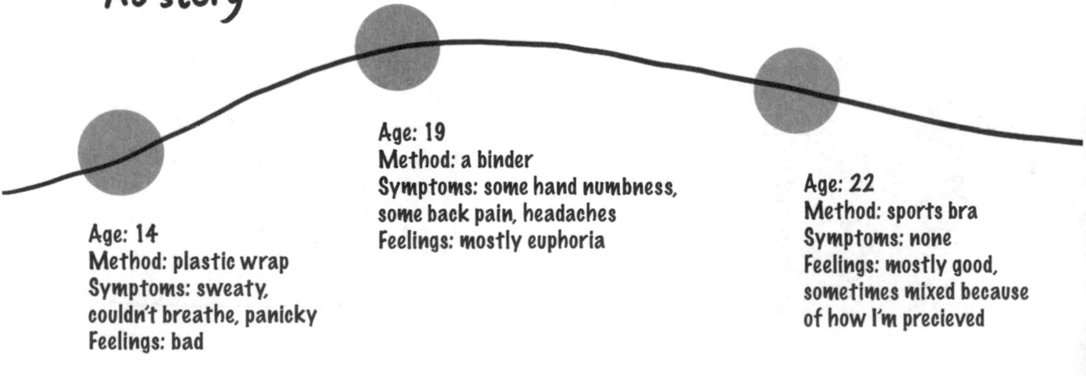
Age: 14
Method: plastic wrap
Symptoms: sweaty, couldn't breathe, panicky
Feelings: bad
Age: 19
Method: a binder
Symptoms: some hand numbness, some back pain, headaches
Feelings: mostly euphoria
Age: 22
Method: sports bra
Symptoms: none
Feelings: mostly good, sometimes mixed because of how I'm precieved

On the last time point, write where you want to take your binding journey next. What method will you use? What symptoms do you hope to decrease? How do you want to feel?

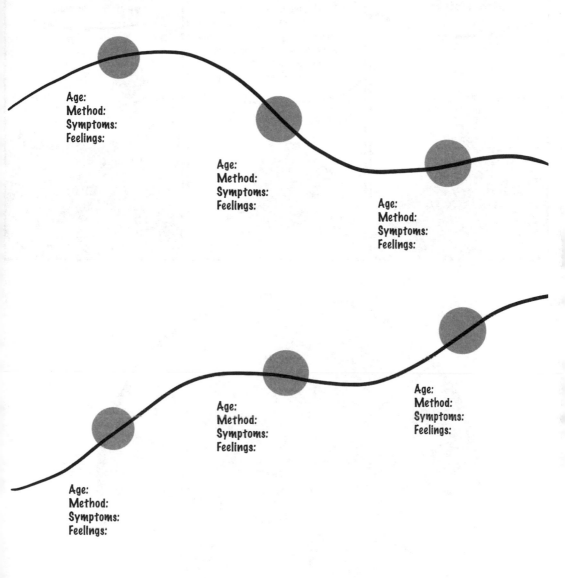

Age:
Method:
Symptoms:
Feelings:

Age:
Method:
Symptoms:
Feelings:

Age:
Method:
Symptoms:
Feelings:

Age:
Method:
Symptoms:
Feelings:

Age:
Method:
Symptoms:
Feelings:

Age:
Method:
Symptoms:
Feelings:

What insights does your timeline spark for you?
Are you binding more or less than you thought? Having more or less symptoms than you thought? What periods of your binding journey were you happiest with? How do you want to see this journey continue in the future?

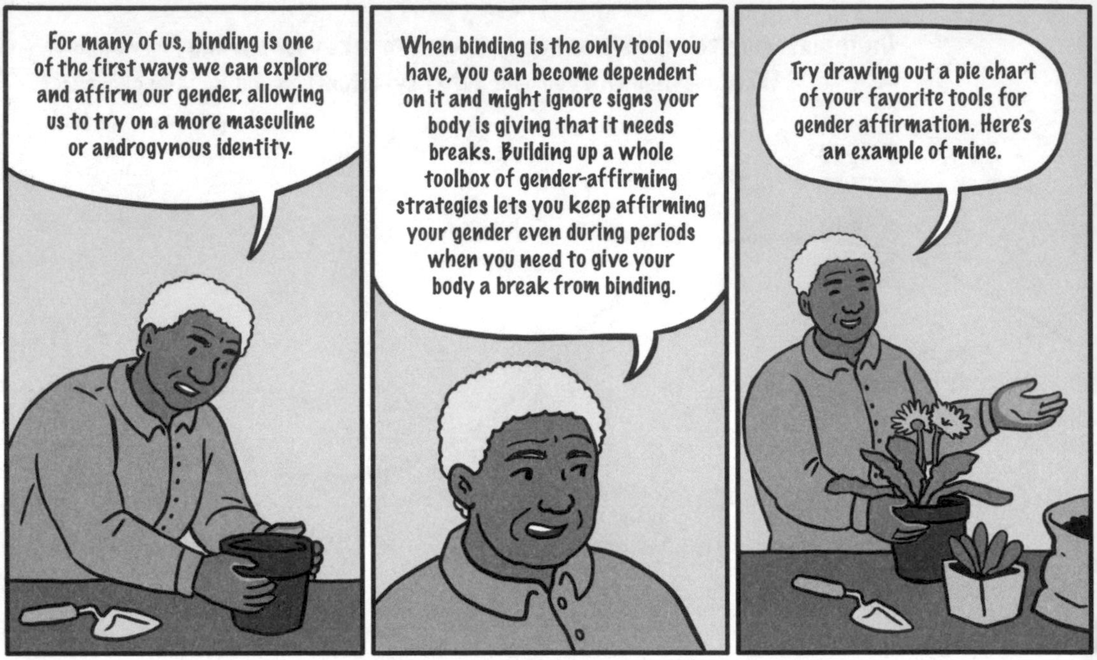
For many of us, binding is one of the first ways we can explore and affirm our gender, allowing us to try on a more masculine or androgynous identity.
When binding is the only tool you have, you can become dependent on it and might ignore signs your body is giving that it needs breaks. Building up a whole toolbox of gender-affirming strategies lets you keep affirming your gender even during periods when you need to give your body a break from binding.
Try drawing out a pie chart of your favorite tools for gender affirmation. Here's an example of mine.

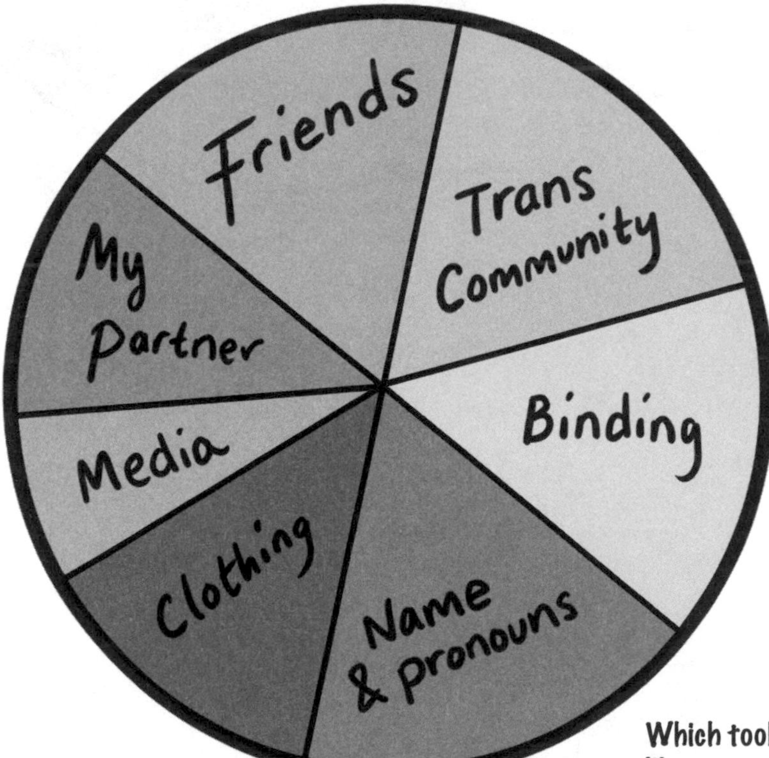
Friends
Trans Community
Binding
Name & pronouns
Clothing
Media
My Partner

Which tools would you like to use more often?

How many slices does your pie chart have right now?

How might you expand your use of that tool?

GENDER VALIDATION PIE CHART

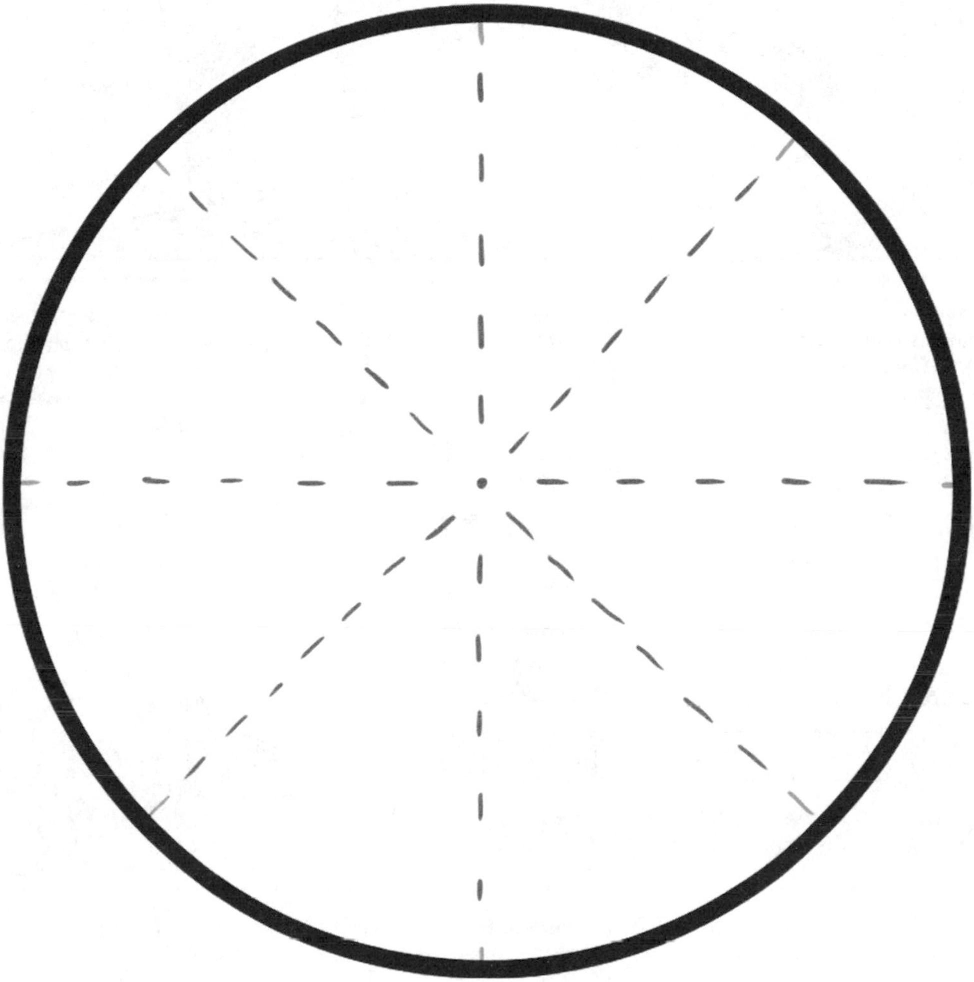

What's one more tool you would really like to add to your toolbox? How might you go about incorporating it into your life?

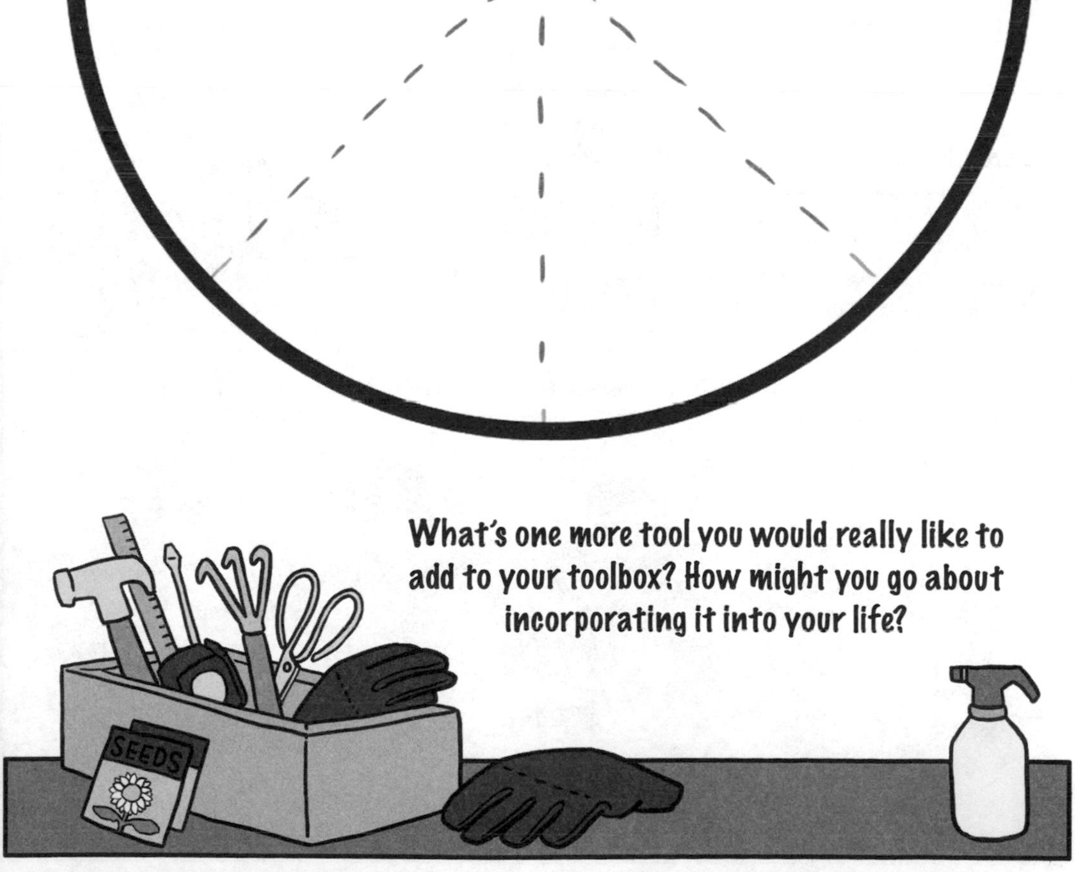
SEEDS

Hello, Sarah here! In addition to the study of 25 people which formed the basis of most of this book, I also ran an earlier study of 1800 participants on their binding habits and associated health effects. We analyzed the data in several papers.

PEDIATRICS Volume 147, Issue 3: "Time to First Onset of Chest Binding-Related Symptoms in Transgender Youth"

TRANGENDER HEALTH Volume 3, Issue 1: "Chest Binding and Care Seeking Among Transmasculine Adults: A Cross-Sectional Study"

CULTURE, HEALTH & SEXUALITY Volume 19, Issue 1: "Health Impact of Chest Binding Among Transgender Adults: A Community-Engaged, Cross-Sectional Study"

We learned that most people who bind do report some symptoms such as overheating, chafing, or headaches. Of our 1800 participants, 97% reported symptoms, but for many the severity was low.

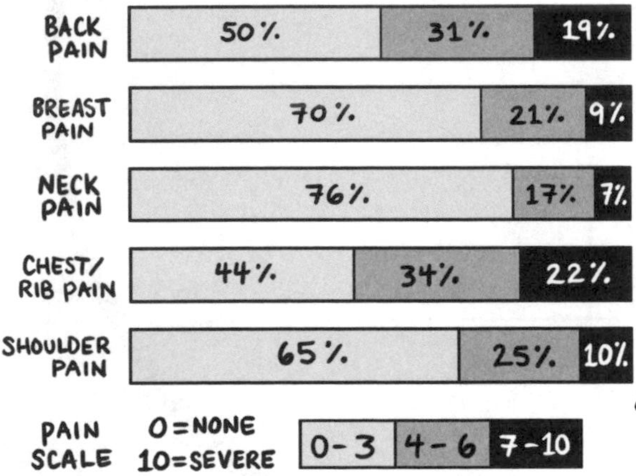

	0–3	4–6	7–10
BACK PAIN	50%	31%	19%
BREAST PAIN	70%	21%	9%
NECK PAIN	76%	17%	7%
CHEST/RIB PAIN	44%	34%	22%
SHOULDER PAIN	65%	25%	10%

PAIN SCALE 0 = NONE 10 = SEVERE

Take shoulder pain, a common symptom. On a scale from 0 to 10, two-thirds of people reported pain at a 3 or lower, which is none to mild shoulder pain. Only 1 in 10 had severe pain.

On the other hand, participants attributed being able to wear a binder to feeling more comfortable in their own skin, and they reported reductions in depression, anxiety, and even suicidality.

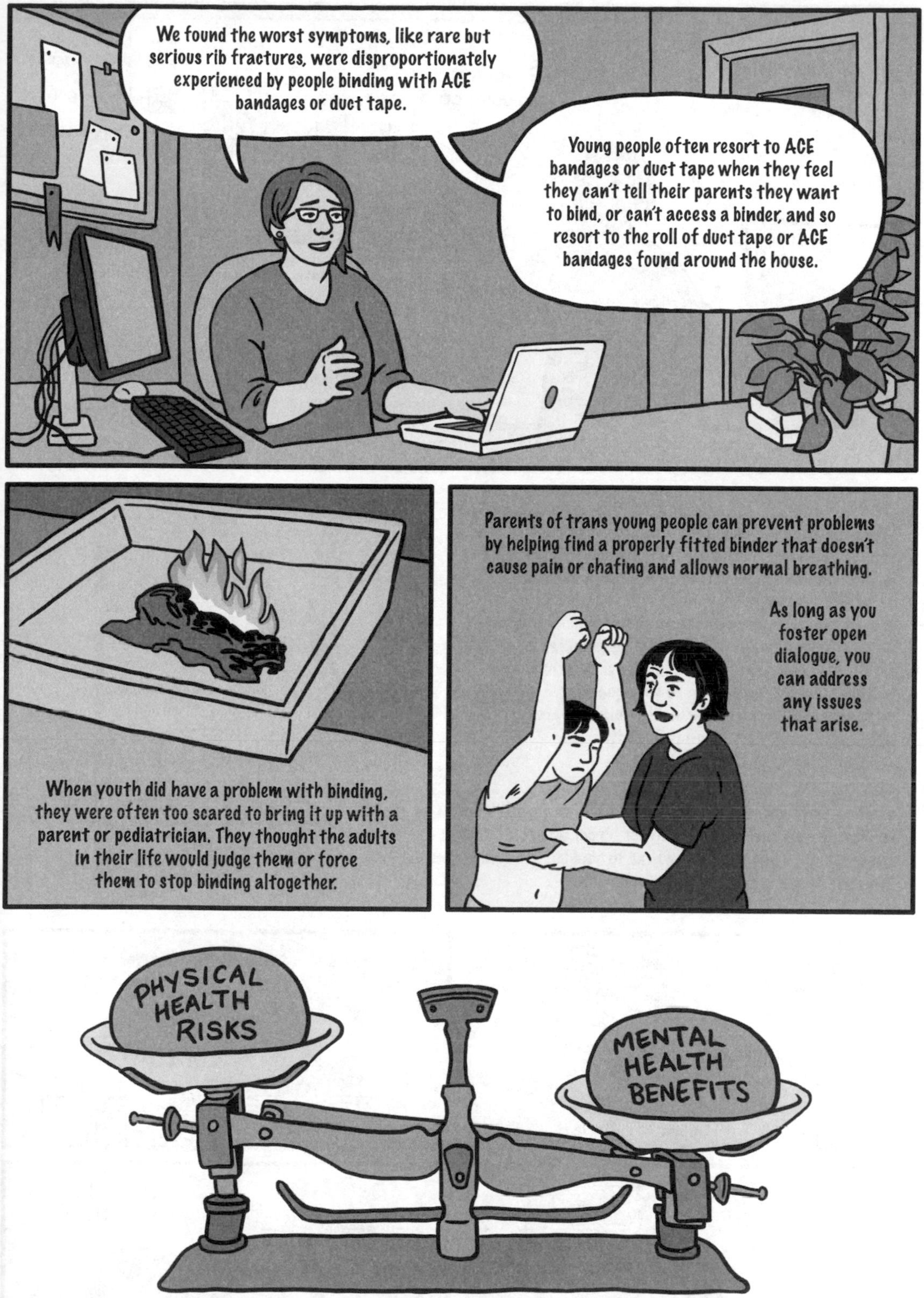
We found the worst symptoms, like rare but serious rib fractures, were disproportionately experienced by people binding with ACE bandages or duct tape.
Young people often resort to ACE bandages or duct tape when they feel they can't tell their parents they want to bind, or can't access a binder, and so resort to the roll of duct tape or ACE bandages found around the house.
When youth did have a problem with binding, they were often too scared to bring it up with a parent or pediatrician. They thought the adults in their life would judge them or force them to stop binding altogether.
Parents of trans young people can prevent problems by helping find a properly fitted binder that doesn't cause pain or chafing and allows normal breathing.
As long as you foster open dialogue, you can address any issues that arise.
PHYSICAL HEALTH RISKS
MENTAL HEALTH BENEFITS

Most people find the physical risks of binding are outweighed by the positive mental health benefits – especially when physical effects can be prevented and minimized by binding using safer methods.

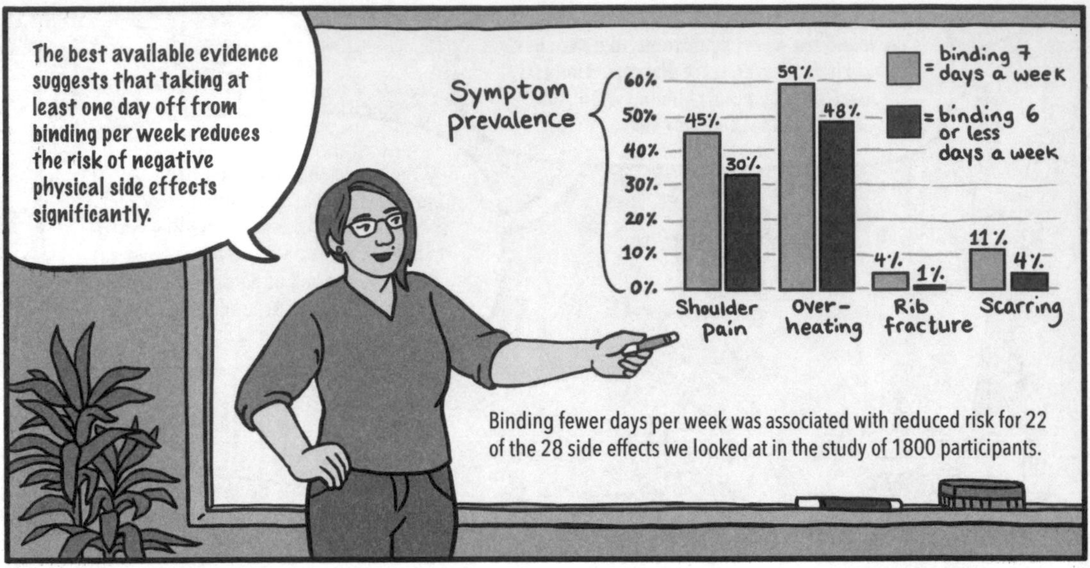
The best available evidence suggests that taking at least one day off from binding per week reduces the risk of negative physical side effects significantly.
Symptom prevalence
60%
50%
40%
30%
20%
10%
0%
45%
30%
59%
48%
4%
1%
11%
4%
Shoulder pain
Over-heating
Rib fracture
Scarring
= binding 7 days a week
= binding 6 or less days a week
Binding fewer days per week was associated with reduced risk for 22 of the 28 side effects we looked at in the study of 1800 participants.

We found that the number of hours per day that someone can safely bind depends on each person's unique body and binding routine. Having a general cutoff like "no more than eight hours per day" is too simplistic – some people can safely bind more, while others may not be able to do eight hours safely. However, binding more hours per day than you need to in order to achieve your goals for mental health, gender affirmation, and/or safety puts unnecessary stress on your body.

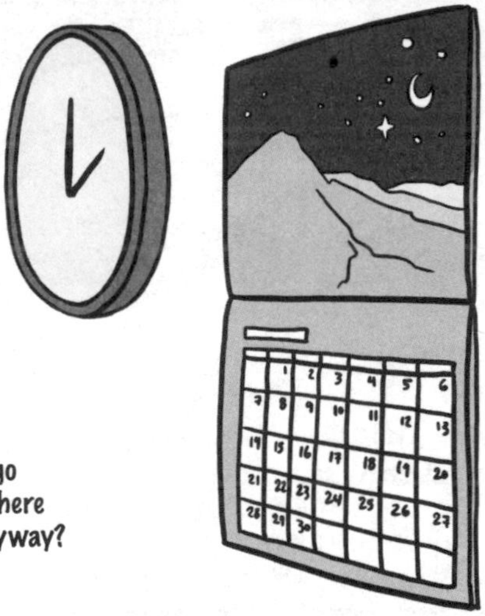

Looking at your daily schedule, are there times when you can go somewhere private to take off your binder and stretch? Are there times when you don't actually need to bind but are doing it anyway? For some people, those times might include:

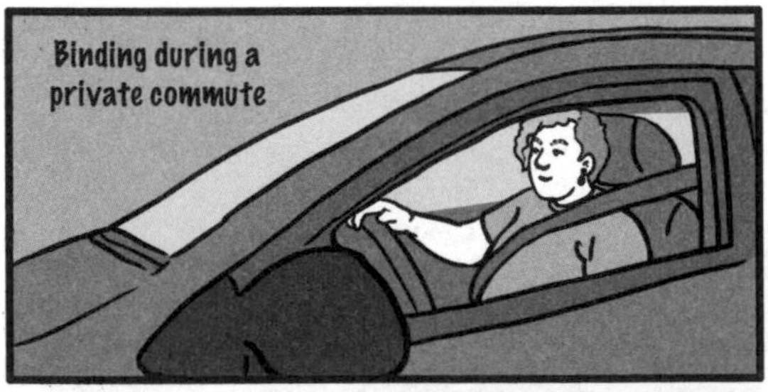
Binding during a private commute

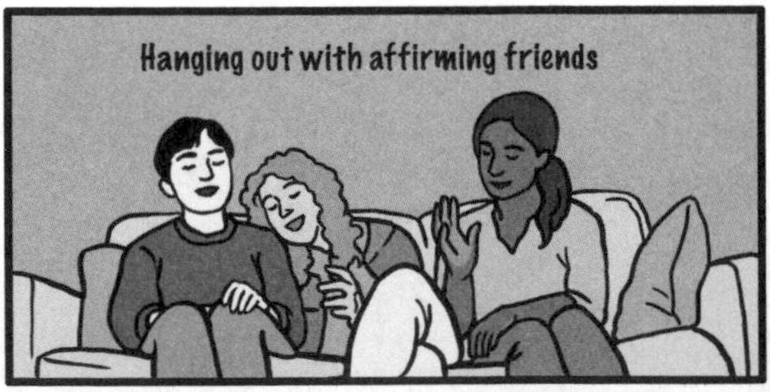
Hanging out with affirming friends

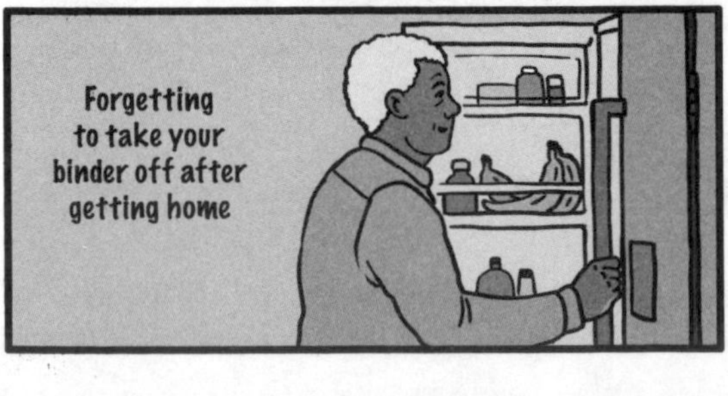
Forgetting to take your binder off after getting home

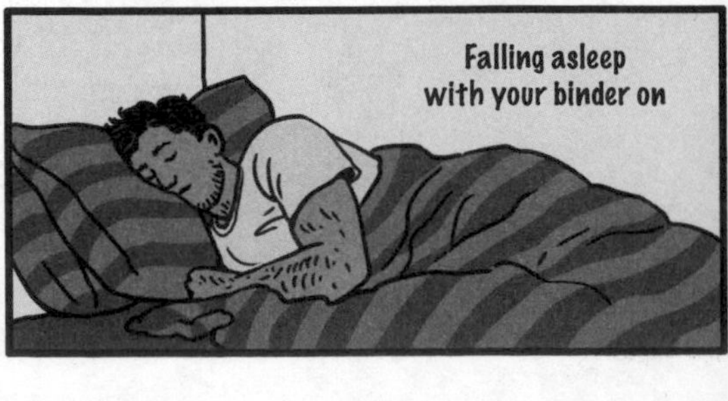
Falling asleep with your binder on

Four out of five people in our study believed it was important to discuss binding symptoms with a healthcare provider, but only 15% had actually done so. The number one predictor of seeing a provider wasn't the severity of symptoms, but rather having a provider with whom they felt safe discussing binding and gender.

Providers can help manage any symptoms that arise, and can also support decision making about whether to use puberty blockers to delay the need to start binding or pursue top surgery, if appropriate and desired, as a way to avoid further binding.

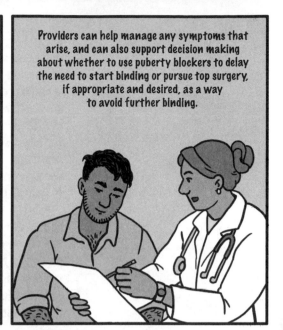

The physical health risks of binding can be prevented or mitigated with safer binding practices, social support, and affirming medical care. The mental health benefits are immediate and tangible – for some, life-changing or even life-saving.

Our studies showed that binding is most dangerous when driven underground by judgment.

We envision a world in which everyone can step into the truth of who they are, not in spite of their health, but in care of it.

Sarah Peitzmeier (she/her), PhD, is an Assistant Professor at the University of Michigan School of Nursing and School of Public Health. Her mixed-methods research focuses on the epidemiology and prevention of gender-based violence, as well as LGBTQ+ health and HIV. She has received funding for her research from the NIH, CDC, and Canadian Institutes of Health Research and is best known for her research to understand, screen for, and intervene to reduce intimate partner violence in transgender populations, as well as her work around the health impacts of chest binding in transmasculine individuals. Her ongoing work includes intervention development studies to prevent campus sexual assault against transgender undergraduates and cisgender women undergraduates. She received her PhD from the Johns Hopkins Bloomberg School of Public Health in 2017.

Kieran Todd (they/them) is a doctoral student in the Department of Social and Behavioral Sciences at the Harvard T.H. Chan School of Public Health. Their work and research focus on addressing structural determinants, primarily racism and cissexism, that are created and sustained by the historical, geographical, and social contexts that influence masculine identity development and health for Black masculine people and those in relationship to them.

Maia Kobabe (e/em/eir) is the author and illustrator of the award-winning and bestselling *Gender Queer: A Memoir*, the most banned book in America in 2021 and 2022. E and eir work have been featured in *Time*, NPR, the *Washington Post*, the *Los Angeles Times*, and many other outlets.

Frances Reed, LMT (they/them) is a licensed massage therapist, author, educator, and binding-health expert. Over the past decade, they have developed techniques for treating and preventing chronic pain in people who bind their chests, which is the subject of their forthcoming book, *Healthy Binding for Trans and Nonbinary People: A Practical Guide*, and their site HealthyBinding.com. In addition to their work on binding, they specialize in top surgery preparation and scar healing. They teach courses on binding health to the community and to health and wellness practitioners.

Meaghan Ray Peters (they/them) is a physiotherapist and a graduate student in Rehabilitation Science at the University of Alberta. They are studying the experiences of people who bind their chests, the symptoms they experience, and how they manage those symptoms. They have been part of the trans community for many years and have a special interest in supporting trans inclusion in the university environment, healthcare system, and research. Follow @chest_binding_support to see the results of their research and for more resources.

Ashley R. Guillory (she/they) is a comics author and storyboard artist whose credits include *The Stand* TV series and *The New Mutants* movie. They colored the cover characters and the interiors of this book. She is also working on several original book pitches focusing on queer love, bodies, health, and pregancy.

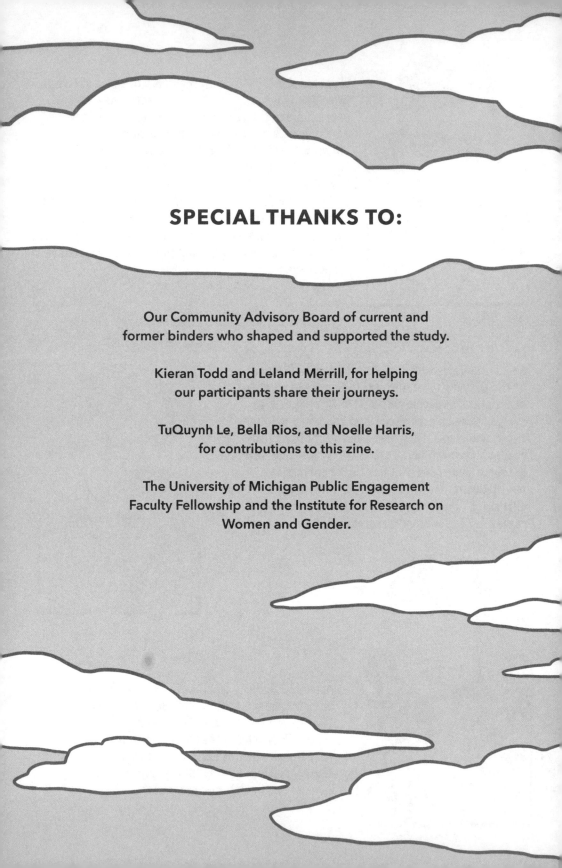

SPECIAL THANKS TO:

Our Community Advisory Board of current and former binders who shaped and supported the study.

Kieran Todd and Leland Merrill, for helping our participants share their journeys.

TuQuynh Le, Bella Rios, and Noelle Harris, for contributions to this zine.

The University of Michigan Public Engagement Faculty Fellowship and the Institute for Research on Women and Gender.